Protection
& Reversal
Magick

Also by Jason Miller:

Consorting with Spirits
The Elements of Spellcrafting
Financial Sorcery
Sex, Sorcery, and Spirit
The Sorcerer's Secrets

Protection & Reversal Magick

A WITCH'S DEFENSE MANUAL

JASON MILLER
(Inominandum)

WEISER BOOKS

This edition first published in 2023 by Weiser Books, an imprint of
Red Wheel/Weiser, LLC
With offices at:
65 Parker Street, Suite 7
Newburyport, MA 01950
www.redwheelweiser.com

ISBN: 978-1-57863-799-7

Library of Congress Cataloging-in-Publication Data

Names: Miller, Jason, 1972- author.
Title: Protection and reversal magick : a witch's defense manual / Jason Miller.
Description: Newburyport : Weiser Books, 2023. | Previously published: Protection
    & reversal magick. Franklin Lakes, N.J. : New Page Books, c2006. | Summary:
    "Everyone, whether they practice witchcraft or not, is susceptible to unwanted
    spells and curses. The difference is that witches and magicians can do something
    about it. Now you can, too. This book is a complete how-to guide to preventing,
    defending, and reversing magical attacks of any kind. These are practical
    techniques for wiccans, witches, ceremonial magicians, root doctors, and anyone
    else who puts magick to a practical use"—Provided by publisher.
Identifiers: LCCN 2022050513 | ISBN 9781578637997 | ISBN 9781633412972
    (kindle edition)
Subjects: LCSH: Witchcraft. | Magic.
Classification: LCC BF1566 .M55 2022 | DDC 133.4/3—dc23/eng/20221212
LC record available at https://lccn.loc.gov/2022050513

Cover design by Sky Peck Design
Cover art © Wojciech Zwolinski/Cambion Art/Arcangel. Used by permission.
Interior images by Matthew Brownlee
Interior design by Debby Dutton
Typeset in Adobe Garamond, Frutiger LT, and Warnock

Printed in the United States of America
IBI

10 9 8 7 6 5 4 3 2 1

For My Beautiful Bride

This is a book of magick meant to be employed in situations of psychic, magick, and spiritual attack. In some cases, these types of occult attacks are accompanied by psychological and medical problems. It is also the case that some people suffering under serious but normal psychological conditions sometimes attribute their illness to magick. I want to make it perfectly clear that no practices presented in this book are meant to replace treatment by medical and psychological professionals. I cannot stress this strongly enough.

Likewise, though some of the protection and counter-magick techniques may prove useful in the case of mundane stalking and threats of physical violence, they should not replace the intervention of police and other appropriate authorities.

There are numerous formulas in the book for incenses, floor washes, spells, and offerings that call for various botanical, mineral, and zoological reagents. Most are harmless, a few are toxic, but none of these formulas are for anything that you are meant to ingest.

Lastly, this is volatile magick, meant to be employed in dire and dangerous circumstances. Should you attempt to help yourself or others using the spells from this book, you should be prepared to accept the consequences of your actions.

Readers using the information in this book do so entirely at their own risk, and the author and publisher accept no liability if adverse effects are caused.

Contents

Acknowledgments

First and foremost, I wish to thank my wife for her patience and encouragement during the writing of this book. I want to thank my family for raising me in an environment that was conducive to learning the magickal arts, and for always encouraging me in my esoteric pursuits, no matter how strange they seemed or how far away they took me.

Thanks to all my initiators, mentors, teachers, friends, and informants who have revealed to me the secrets of their crafts. Special thanks for this go to: John Myrdhin Reynolds, Namkhai Norbu, Lopon Tenzin Namdak, Kunzang Dorje Rinpoche, Cliff and Misha Pollick, catherine yronwode, Tau Nemesius, Paul Hume, Lama Wangdor, Frater Xanthias, Matt Brownlee, Alfred Vitale, B. Gendler, Al Billings, Blanch Krubner, Dr. Jim, Howard and Amy Wuelfing, and Susan Vuono. My thanks also go to all the members of Thelesis Oasis in Philadelphia, the Old Snake Cabal, the Chthonic Auranian Temple, the Terra Sancta Sodality, the Wild Hunt Club, and Ngakpa Zhonnu Khang for their continued fraternity and support.

Lastly, I must thank the many gods and spirits who have been invoked in the text and during the writing of the book. In particular I want to acknowledge Papa Legba, who blessed this work and opened many doors during the course of its writing; and the Goddess Hekate, patroness of this book.

Preface

A WORD ABOUT THE
MAGICK IN THIS BOOK

This book is an attempt to step beyond the "101s" that seem to fill the shelves these days. Although it is assumed that the reader already knows a little bit about witchcraft and magick, I want to take a moment to define terms and talk about approaches taken to the magick in the book, which may be different from what you are used to.

The first thing I want to make clear is that this is a book on defensive witchcraft, not Wicca. Though many use the terms interchangeably, witchcraft embraces a much wider spectrum than just Wicca, which can be seen as a particular type of religious witchcraft. Witchcraft, as we use the term in this book, is a *craft* and implies a type of practical sorcery and mysticism that embraces elements of the chthonic, lunar, feminine, and so on in its practice. As Robert Cochrane said when he was asked what a witch is:

> If one who claims he or she is a witch can perform the tasks
> of witchcraft, that is they can summon spirits and spirits
> will come, they can turn hot into cold and cold into hot,

they can divine with rod, fingers, and birds, they can claim the right to omens and have them. Above all they can tell the Maze and cross the Lethe. If they can do these things, then you have a witch.[1]

The magick in this book is certainly applicable to Wiccans and Pagans, but it could just as easily be employed by ceremonial magicians, rootworkers, or anyone else who embraces the basic principles of operative witchcraft.

To avoid rehashing the same old rituals that have been explained time and time again, I have endeavored to make the spells and rites in this book as original as I can. That said, I have been trained in traditional magicks from all over the world and many will recognize the traditional roots of my rituals. Because this is a book on practical magick, I have made no effort to focus on one tradition at the exclusion of another. Thus you will find spells that have their roots in African-American hoodoo, alongside ones inspired by European folk magick, and ones that stem from Himalayan Tantric Sorcery. Tech is tech after all, and what works is what works, be it magick or machinery. As Aleister Crowley said, "Success be thy proof."

Lastly, I have dedicated this work to the Goddess Hekate in all her many diverse forms. Most of the spoken spells and incantations invoke her or spirits connected to her. These spoken incantations can be altered or replaced to fit individual disposition, taste, and tradition without changing the overall nature of the spell. Some people like rhyming couplets, some find them silly. Some will be moved by incantations in Latin and Greek, some insist on working only in English. Take these rituals as a base and make them your own. In doing so, you are participating in the true tradition of cunning men and wise women throughout history, which keeps the craft a living tradition instead of a collection of static litanies.

Introduction
to the New Edition

Let me tell you about how this book came into being.

Back in the halcyon days of 2005 there was a website called Witchvox that had monthly themes. I can't remember the exact topic I responded to, but it had to do with spells and their relationship to witchcraft. The site was absolutely overflowing with short articles assuring everyone that no one needed to bother with proper herbs or instructions or really anything at all other than their intention. No matter what books or history or tradition teaches, these articles assured readers that whatever they think is right is all that matters.

Piling on to this mountain of bad ideas was an article by a well-known Pagan author, Carl McColman, who felt that not only were spells ineffective at achieving any real results, but that they actually distract from the authentic spiritual teachings Paganism as a religion had to offer.

I never submitted anything to Witchvox before, but I had to present at least one dissenting voice against what I saw as a dismissal of magick itself. Someone. Someone had to say that witches and magicians of the past did not painstakingly record spellbooks and formularies because intention was all that mattered. Someone had to say that no, writing the word "galangal" on a piece of paper and dropping it in a mojo bag was not the same thing as actually using galangal root. Most of all, someone had to say that if you want to look for the ancient roots of witchcraft, the literal *craft* done by witches, it is best found by examining the rich tradition of spell work, not in religions that were largely made up in the 20th century.

My screed caught the attention of one of McColman's publishers, New Page Books, who reached out to me to see if I wanted to write a book. I said yes, of course. I wanted to write on a topic that I thought people were not taking seriously enough at the time. *Protection and Reversal Magick* was born.

Carl, by the way, converted to Catholicism and is one of my very favorite writers on Catholic Mysticism. If you want to know about Christian contemplative traditions, I cannot recommend his books and website highly enough. If, however, you want to ask about how to get Saint Martha to dominate your boss at work, or how to do a Novena to Saint Sara for divination skills, you are better off asking someone else, because those are just as much spells as anything else is.

So, my little book is now sixteen years old. Red Wheel/Weiser purchased New Page Books and here I am trying to update my thoughts. Rather than mess around with the content of a book that has served so many so well, I have opted to include notes at the end of each chapter. There is, however, one big issue that needs to be addressed head on.

When I wrote this book in 2006, I felt people were not taking magick very seriously. I would regularly encounter the idea any "real" witch doesn't curse because of the law of Karma. Some told me that they were immune from psychic attack because they banish daily or wear a pentagram for protection. Most teachers would reflexively write off anyone who claimed to be jinxed, cursed, attacked, or suffering crossed conditions as either delusional or prone to drama.

Having grown up around not only Pagans and ceremonial magicians, but rootworkers, bokors, and other assorted strains of sorcerers, I knew that people did in fact place curses on others from time to time. Items for curses were hot sellers at the botanicas and conjure shops I frequented. Not only that but spirits themselves can be the source of psychic attacks and crossed conditions when offended.

I originally wrote this book to say that magickal attacks and crossed conditions are very real, and it's wrong to dismiss them out of hand. I wanted to provide tools that would help realistically assess, protect against, and, if necessary, reverse these forces.

If the goal was to get the overall community to take psychic, spiritual, and magickal attack seriously, I can say, sixteen years later, that I was successful. Maybe a little too successful.

Currently in 2022 it seems to me that a good deal of the Pagans, witches, and magicians I meet now are strangely terrified of the magick they do. People summon spirits, then panic when spirits show up. Witches burn candles at midnight and freak out if the melted wax looks ominous. They call upon underworld spirits and then think they they are being attacked from multiple sources but can give no solid reason.

So since I get to update this introduction, let's pull it back a bit. It is still true that magickal attacks and spirit obsessions happen. That doesn't mean that they happen all the time for no good reason.

Being the victim of a psychic or magickal attack is an attractive proposition for two reasons: it makes you important enough to be cursed but also frees you from any responsibility for bad things in life. Being at the center of drama always bolsters the ego. I mean, if people are spending their time cursing you, you must be important, right? That sense of importance is, in a strange way, an ego boost. Of course, if you are under attack, you have something to blame for anything going wrong in life. You can tell yourself that you lost your job because you are the victim of a curse, not because you showed up late unprepared and looking like an unmade bed.

Often someone who suspects that they are cursed or suffering crossed conditions will seek out a reading. The reader will say, *Yes, I see a curse,* then spin a yarn about how their aunt is cursing them. Then they go see another reader who confirms that they are indeed cursed, but it's a shaman whose workshop they attended a few months ago. A third reader also verifies the curse, but suggests that it's an ancestral curse. Rather than consider the idea that at least two of these readers are wrong, or only partially correct, the victim will excitedly tell people how they are being actively cursed by their aunt, a shaman, and someone their ancestors ticked off in 1789. See the problem here?

Because I am an author, several times a year people send me emails accusing me of cursing them. Whether they were told this through divination or just gossipy fantasy, that's what they have been told and what they now believe. Let me tell you a secret: the number of people that I have cursed in the last sixteen years is ZERO. I don't even know who most of these people are, but it does illustrate how attractive the fantasy of being cursed can be.

There have always been people like this, though. Both people eager to be the victim of a curse and those jumping at the chance to save them from their fate. What troubles me more than people believing that they are cursed when they aren't is an overall growing fear I see in the community. I regularly encounter students who live in terror of missing a day of prayer or offering, lest the God that they have chosen to propitiate wreck their life. I have talked to conjurors who won't conjure because they are afraid that they won't be able to dismiss what they summon. Last month I talked with someone who had been calling themselves a witch for two years but was scared to do a spell lest it "backfire."

Reasonable precautions are good, but knee-jerk fears are not helpful.

I am assuming that everyone reading this knows that magick doesn't work like it does in Harry Potter or Dungeons and Dragons. Well, it doesn't work like it does in horror movies, either. Think about it—if the magick is strong enough to call a spirit into your presence, why would you assume it's not strong enough to dismiss that spirit? Unless you choose to believe that all magick is some incredibly elaborate plot to trick people into becoming possessed, it doesn't make much sense, does it? If that's what you think, then what are you even doing messing around in magick?

Are there spirits who might cause you harm? Sure. Just like there are people that might cause you harm. Are all or even most spirits inherently dangerous? No. Again, just like people.

I am almost fifty years old, so the people I learned from are now hitting their seventies and eighties. Most of them have been summoning spirits, communicating with angels, and even making pacts with demons since I was a teenager. They are doing fine. Remarkably well, in fact. No great tragedy beyond those normal for old age, bad economy, and crumbling environment.

So, am I saying that it's safe then? That there is no danger? *Not at all.* This kind of either/or thinking never serves anyone very well. Magick is real and anything real has dangers, which brings me back to the introduction I wrote for the first edition. It's a bit like driving a car: it's dangerous, but you decide that the benefits are worth the risks. You wear a seat belt and learn safety precautions, and everything goes well most of the time despite the risks. Sometimes you have a problem or an accident. Rarely something catastrophic happens.

Reasonable risks that you can never fully eliminate no matter how careful you are or how many precautions you take are how you are already living your life. I wrote this book to give you better protections and protocols, not to sow fear and paranoia.

May the knowledge in the book aid you in staying safe on your journey, but also remind you that there is no such thing as being completely safe.

Jason Miller
Beltane 2022

Introduction

We live in a dangerous world. Setting aside magick and witchcraft for the moment, everything we do has an element of danger to it, no matter how small. Every time you get behind the wheel of a car, or travel to a new place, or let a new person know where you live, you are flirting with danger. With a few paranoid exceptions, most of us accept these dangers and go on with our lives. The reason that we are able to do so without being afraid is that we take reasonable precautions. We buckle our seat belts, we learn to judge people, and we know how to contact the authorities if needed. The world is dangerous, but we deal with it.

Certain occupations and activities increase the danger in your life. A police officer or a skydiver lives a more dangerous life than an office worker. They take extra precautions to deal with the specific dangers of their occupations. In some cases, such as a police officer, he helps others in need deal with their own danger.

The path of a magician or witch also has its own dangers. Paul Huson, in his book *Mastering Witchcraft*, warned, "The moment that you set foot upon the path of witchcraft, a call rings out in the unseen world announcing your arrival." Not everything that hears this call will have your best interests at heart. In order to make the craft more acceptable to mainstream culture, many modern books on the craft understate any dangers or pretend that there are none at all. If you are one of the few who actually go beyond reading books and attending festivals and actually get your hands dirty practicing the craft of magick, you will most assuredly find that at some point in your practice it will be necessary to defend yourself against occult forces that have been set against you. I would, in fact, argue that magickal and psychic attack occurs far more frequently than many suspect.

Not only may you have to deal with occult, psychic, and spiritual attacks on yourself, but, like a police officer, a witch is sometimes called upon to intercede against these forces on the behalf of others. The role of protector and exorcist is one of the oldest societal roles for magicians and is still played out today in traditional cultures. I have noted that the phrases "cunning man" and "cunning woman" are enjoying a renaissance in certain quarters of the craft these days. What's interesting and somewhat ironic about this is that the historical cunning man would have actually been in the business of combating witchcraft! Of course, the "witchcraft" that they would detect and rout was not the result of a particular religion, such as Wicca, but rather any type of psychic, spiritual, or magickal attack. They would have had a professional practice to which someone could turn if he felt that malefica was being aimed at them. These cunning men and women, the genuine ones, were indeed witches themselves. Though not necessarily Pagan, they were practitioners of folk and ritual magick.

I am convinced that the ability to identify, protect against, and reverse occult attack is just as relevant for witches and sorcerers today as it was for the cunning man of old. Never before has there been so much magickal and occult knowledge readily available to the public. Never before have so many stumbled so cavalierly into arcane practices that were once closely guarded secrets. While some introductory books hold that the dangers of the occult are few and magickal attacks are rare, experience has taught me otherwise. Whether crossed conditions brought on by our own magickal missteps, intrusions from obsessive spirits, or deliberate attacks from other magicians and witches, I have found that magickal attack happens far more often than even most occultists realize. In fact, as a professional sorcerer, many of the people who contact me in need of magickal defense are themselves magicians and witches of one kind or another, who simply had no idea they would ever have a problem that couldn't be wished away with good thoughts and a few pentagrams drawn in the air.

We are all meant for different things. During the years that I have spent studying the occult and practicing magick, it has become apparent to me that part of my destiny, or *karma,* involves helping people defend against magickal attack and spirit obsession. Long before I ever made my services public, people sought me out for help with these types of problems. Because of this, I have made it a point to study the methods of exorcism, counter-magick, protection, and reversing in every magickal system I have encountered, from European witchcraft and high magick, to Himalayan Tantra, to old-fashioned American hoodoo.

I have been on the receiving end of magickal attacks and know the paranoia, frustration, and terror that they can cause. I have also laid curses and jinxes upon others when I felt that justified reasons arose, and so I know the mindset of an attacker and the repercussions of using offensive magick. I have not gained this knowledge without cost, and I anticipate that there will be cost in its sharing, though what this will be I do not yet know.

I am not suggesting that everyone needs to specialize in this aspect of the craft, and I certainly do not want to make anyone paranoid about potential dangers, but if you are to practice magick, you should be able to make reasonable defense against attacks and deal with problems when they arise. If I can provide knowledge to this end, then I will have fulfilled my purpose.

As the mages of ancient Egypt said, "Cheper en emdo jen, shesep en heka-o jen" ("May your words occur, may your magick shine!").

Chapter 1

RECOGNIZING ATTACK

SOURCES OF ATTACK

Because this book is about magickal defense, the first question that must be answered is: Who or what are we defending ourselves against? In my experience, occult attack and crossed conditions generally stem from one of four sources: (1) offended spirits acting in retribution for offensive actions; (2) people stumbling unprepared into places of power and being negatively affected by their ambience; (3) missteps or broken vows in our occult practice; and (4) attacks from other practitioners.

Offended Spirits

Humans are not alone in this world. The planet is a living organism, and many traditional cultures recognize that all space is permeated by awareness and energy. By living in a thoughtless and contrary way with our environment, we can come into conflict with various intelligences and spirits that share our space. Our worlds overlap, and though we cannot perceive each other's presence easily, we do affect each other. Through burning and dumping waste, damming up rivers and lakes, building cities, and performing other actions in which we disturb the natural environment, we run the risk of upsetting these spiritual beings and earning their wrath. A large portion of traditional medicine and shamanism in indigenous cultures is geared toward addressing maladies caused by these spirits.

When I lived in Nepal I had an acquaintance that became gravely and inexplicably ill. The hospital couldn't figure out what was wrong, and it was suggested that he go see a doctor of Tibetan medicine. The doctor realized that he had upset a group of Nagas, chthonic serpent spirits, by bathing in a particular pool during a hike. He was given some medicine for the symptoms, but beyond treating the symptoms, it was more important for him to have the spirits exorcised and for him to make offerings and ask forgiveness of this group of spirits. He did, and he got better soon afterward. Because the spirits are made of energy and awareness, they can affect us on those subtle layers and filter the effect into the physical levels of our immune and nervous system. They can also affect our emotional disposition and thought process. For instance, another group of spirits in the Himalayas called the Gyalpos are known to be fond of exciting hate and anger and are thought to be the cause of several wars.

Though the modern world does not recognize these dangers, all magickal paradigms have some way of dealing with them. Far from being the providence only of tribal shamans in Asia and Africa, the witches of old Europe prescribed plenty of remedies against incursions from the spirits, as did the medieval grimoires of ceremonial magick. For instance, in the Testament of Solomon, which is the basis for many famous grimoires, such as the Goetia, we are given a list of demons that cause various ailments and the angelic forces that drive them off:

So I put to them the question: "Who are ye called?" The first said: "I, O Lord, am called Ruax, and I cause the heads of men to be idle, and I pillage their brows. But let me only hear the words, 'Michael, imprison Ruax,' and at once I retreat."

And the second said: "I am called Barsafael, and I cause those who are subject to my hour to feel the pain of migraine. If only I hear the words, 'Gabriel, imprison Barsafael,' at once I retreat."

The third said: "I am called Arôtosael. I do harm to eyes, and grievously injure them. Only let me hear the words, 'Uriel, imprison Aratosael' [sic], at once I retreat."

Occult Ambience

Given that we can attract the ire of spirits just by living our everyday lives, it stands to reason that the problem is greatly compounded when we stumble upon places of power where great amounts of occult force are concentrated or that are haunted by disturbed presences. Because our modern world has largely shut us off from our natural psychic sensitivity, most people will wander through these places without noticing anything peculiar. However, some people who are just a little sensitive to these forces can find that sensitivity increases in an uncomfortably drastic manner in certain places and circumstances, and thus we come to our second source of attack: occult ambience. There are many stories of people being "touched" by places dedicated to spirit. If a beautiful temple or circle of trees can inspire us by its power, then it stands to reason that certain places will touch us in the opposite way, disturbing our energy and bringing us into contact with malefic forces.

These places can be naturally powerful because of a gathering of geo-psychic energy, such as at a ley-line nexus or a fairy mound, but they can also be places empowered by the actions of humans, such as ancient shrines, graveyards, or places where something psychically potent once happened, such as a murder or rape, or even a séance that was performed long ago. Whatever the cause of the potency, such places can ignite the psychic potential in people that spend time in them. Without training and guidance, the sudden change in awareness will come as a shock and leave someone vulnerable to forces that they never even knew existed. Even if the powers are benign, the shift in perception may simply be too much to handle.

If ordinary people are unknowingly troubled by spirits and the "powers that be" for infringing upon the unseen world accidentally, it stands to reason that the sorcerer, who makes a life out of contact with the unseen, is confronted with such dangers even more often. The difference is that the witch is in a position to do something about it! There is an old cliché in magick that warns: "Do not call up that which you cannot put down." The problem with this advice is that it is hard to figure out exactly what you can put down until you take a chance in calling it up. We could play it safe by not summoning up anything at all, but most occultists seek to grow in knowledge and power by finding their limits and pushing past them.

Though there is a stigma on certain classically Faustian practices such as evocation and necromancy, it is vital to know that even common practices, such as casting circles, scrying, divining, and raising power, can light up the astral plane and make us more noticeable to denizens of the subtle realms. This in turn increases our chances of attracting malefic or mischievous energies amidst all the other beings that we will encounter. Naturally, the more advanced and experimental you are with magick, the greater the potential for a misstep, but some people can run into problems even doing very basic work. Indeed, experience has taught me that some people with emotional problems and mental illness take up magick to seek help with their problems only to find that the problem is exacerbated by even rudimentary banishing practices!

Broken Vows

Apart from experimentation, there is another way our own practice can turn against us that surprisingly few people consider: that is the breaking of magickal vows. Vows made during initiations, self-empowerment ceremonies, or even solitary promises made to the gods and spirits outside of formal ritual will rebound upon us and manifest as an attack if broken. To cite an example from my own life, when I was just seventeen years old I was working my way through Donald Michael Kraig's excellent textbook *Modern Magick*, and I decided it was time to perform his "Ritual of Magickal Obligation," which is based upon the Oath of an Adeptus Minor from the Hermetic Order of the Golden Dawn. In the obligation I vowed to do several things, amongst which were the promises not to display my magickal tools to nonpractitioners, not to lie, and not to spread rumors. In my youthful exuberance I made these promises in the presence of the gods and spirits, and then promptly broke them. I felt the repercussion the moment I told my first lie to my boss at work a few days after taking the obligation. My spells stopped working for a time, and I noted a definite lack of vitality. To fix the situation I created another rite of apology and offering, renouncing the former vow. I do not wish to denigrate the practice of taking vows. Since then, I have taken several magickal vows both solitary and to various groups, and I have benefited greatly from keeping them, but I am now very discerning with what I agree to. When powerful guardians of a current coven, or magickal order are invoked in the vows, the problem can escalate a situation from simple crossed conditions such as I experienced, to outright attacks from the guardians that once protected you. Be careful what you agree to.

Attacks from Other Practitioners

The last source of danger we need to be concerned with, and the one that the majority of this book is focused on, is attacks from other magicians, witches, and psychics. I have seen it written that no *real* witch would ever do magick to harm someone or influence another's will. I have seen it argued that no *genuine* ceremonial magician would harm another because he knows that the law of karma would turn his work back upon him. I have also heard the argument that anyone with the power it takes to launch a successful magickal attack would be evolved enough to be beyond doing such things. All I have to say is: don't you believe it! Such arguments help sell books and help make witchcraft more acceptable to mainstream society, but it's just wishful thinking on the part of people who should know better.

It is comforting to think that all witches adhere to a moral code such as the Wiccan Rede and because of that never would harm anyone, but it's simply not the case. In fact, if we take into account the full spectrum of practitioners of magick and witchcraft, I can assure you that comparatively few hold true to these rules. Any owner of a well-stocked occult supply store can tell you that items geared toward harmful and coercive magick are hot sellers! Like pornography, it's something that no one ever admits to doing, but still seems to be done by an awful lot of folks.

From the Greek defixiones tablets that were prepared to jinx races, force a lover's obedience, and do in enemies; to Mabel Brigge's "Black Fast" in the 1500s; to Doctor Buzzard in Georgia laying Goofer Dust against his clients' foes; a perusal of magickal practices throughout world history will show that curses and bindings have always been a part of witchcraft in the past, and remain so to this day. Just a few months before I wrote this, a group of Kabalistic sorcerers in Israel gathered at an ancient cemetery to perform the

Pulsa Dinura, or Lashes of Fire curse, against Ariel Sharon.[1] Sharon died in 2014.

We must not think that only evil people with no morals engage in such activities either. Most practitioners have the same rules for magick that they do for any other type of action. If they would use mundane means to get revenge, cause harm, confuse, or influence another person, then chances are they will feel comfortable using magick to achieve the same ends. I have even seen strident "white lighters" jump to curses when they feel that their cause is just or that they are serving a greater good. The catch, of course, is that most people *always* feel that their actions are justified and will use all sorts of reasoning to arrive at that conclusion.

Even if you don't practice magick yourself, you can hire a professional to send a curse for you. While most professional workers these days (myself included) shun accepting this type of work without some good cause, there are those who will take any job for a price. In most traditional cultures, it would be a fairly common thing to approach a witch and ask for someone to be jinxed or cursed, and would be just as common to approach someone to take it off. There have even been a few documented cases of one conjurer working both sides of the fence on the same client, laying the curse and then taking it off!

What complicates matters is that not every curse is intentional. It is well known that gifted people can manifest powerful hexes without any training or intent. In Italy, for instance, Maloccio, the "evil eye," is generally thought to be cast through the sheer power of envy, hatred, or simple ill-wishing. Anyone with enough power, a sufficient emotional charge, and a target can launch an accidental psychic attack. It is also possible that people of weak constitution or will can become psychic parasites, unintentionally draining those around them of vitality. Though these attacks are accidental, they need to be dealt with all the same.

IDENTIFYING ATTACK

If we are vigilant in keeping up regular banishing rituals and protections, most of the time we will be fine. In fact, if you are keeping up with the practices in the next chapter, you will be better than fine, because not only are you protecting yourself from unwanted magickal influences, but you are also strengthening your mind and spirit in general. There are times, however, that those protections will not be enough and some kind of attack, accidental or intentional, will get through our defenses and affect our health, our luck, and our general well-being. It is not a pleasant experience, but recognizing an attack when it happens is the first step to combating it.

The first problem that we have is that people generally do not want to admit that an attack is happening. People who don't practice magick are probably more likely to think that they are going crazy than to think that they are under magickal attack. Even if they do suspect occult reasons for their troubles, they won't want to tell anyone for fear of not being believed or earning a reputation as mentally unbalanced.

Sometimes even magicians have a hard time admitting that they are under attack. Many tend to overestimate their abilities or think that whatever regular protections they use are infallible. It is an ego blow to admit that someone or something could get to us, and so we convince ourselves otherwise. This is particularly true if you are in a leadership or teaching position in a magickal group, where you may fear people will not see you as qualified if you admit to being the victim of an attack.

I know a priestess with thirty years of practice under her belt who was attacked a few years back by her lover's ex-wife. I don't want to paint the tradition the ex-wife followed as evil, because it is not, but it is safe to say that it would be not uncommon in that tradition to curse someone out of jealousy. My priestess friend fell severely ill, lost her job, lost her students, and damn near lost her house. She had all the signs of psychic attack, even a very probable source with a motive, but refused to recognize it because she thought of herself as an accomplished witch who was beyond the touch of someone else's curse. She eventually came around, and things are getting better for her.

In general, I think it's good to keep two things in mind. The first is that no one is impervious to psychic attack of some kind. Basic banishings, shields, and amulets will protect you from most accidental psychic attacks and general malefic energies that you may encounter. They will even protect you from most intentional magickal attacks, but no technique is foolproof. No matter what level of initiation you possess and how powerful you think you are, you are not impervious and should bear that in mind. The second thing to keep in mind is that there is no harm in defending against an attack that may not be happening, but great harm can come from ignoring a real attack that you tell yourself isn't happening. Play it on the safe side.

Of course, just as there are people who read medical textbooks and convince themselves that they have every disease in the book, there will be psychic hypochondriacs who read this book and fantasize that they are under attack for no reason. In fact, there are some people who seem to think that they are constantly under attack. These people may come to you seeking help, but they are easy to spot.

There is usually an inverse relationship between the insistence that someone is being magickally attacked and the probability that they actually are. Whether due to actual delusion or just a desire to add a bit of drama to their lives through playing out psychic soap operas, these folks are best avoided. You may not be able to tell who these folks are at first, but you will soon realize their pattern when they keep coming back complaining of new attacks from unknown "black lodges" and "dark magicians." Of course, none of these groups would have any reason to spend energy attacking this person, except for the sheer evil of it, which seems like a good enough reason to the hypochondriac.

If you run into these folks, you can offer them a simple cleansing or some shielding instructions, perhaps an amulet just in case, but they usually keep coming back again and again. These folks are best let down gently by doing divinations and declaring that you can't help them because you cannot detect the source of an attack. You aren't outright contradicting their beliefs, just saying that you aren't in a position to help.

SYMPTOMS OF ATTACK

When it does happen, spiritual attack can manifest its symptoms in numerous ways and varying strength. I divide symptoms into three basic categories: external conditions, mental conditions, and physical conditions.

External Conditions

Attacks of this nature affect the probabilities of events, or luck, in a person's life, creating what is known as "crossed conditions." This often starts by a mild feeling of being out of step with time, as if you can no longer manage to be in the right place at the right time. No matter what you do, you find that you can't seem to get anywhere on time. This can be accompanied by patterns of bad luck, and of everything you touch going wrong. Not just one fender bender in your car, but several in the space of a few days. Things breaking apart in your hands or falling when you try to grab them are common symptoms as well. People don't seem to have any patience with you. Unexpected bills start piling up and you can't seem to hang onto money.

Left alone, things get worse: you lose your job, your lover leaves you, you wreck the car, you are blamed for something you didn't do, and perhaps even wind up in jail or worse. The possibilities of what can happen are limited only by the power of the person or power launching the attack, and how long you let it go on.

Just recently I received three traffic tickets all within two weeks. This was after many years of never getting pulled over. A few other things had been going wrong as well, and I started to suspect something was wrong. After some readings and careful thought, I discovered that it was an accidental attack by someone for whom I refused to do a favor. I did a simple uncrossing, and the problem corrected itself, but the person was strong enough of a psychic that their ill-wishing got through my normal defenses. If I hadn't acted, the crossed conditions could have grown much worse.

Almost everything that happens will have a completely rational and material explanation. Taken alone, they don't mean anything. Taken together, a long string of unfortunate coincidences should be a good indicator that something is amiss. This is especially true if these external conditions are accompanied by some of the mental and physical symptoms listed here.

Mental Conditions

A Santera I know was having problems with her neighbor being loud and obnoxious at all hours of the night and leaving garbage on her lawn. She asked her madrina (her teacher) what she should do. The madrina told her to make a doll that looked like the neighbor, blindfold it, tie its arms and legs, and nail it to the tree in her yard facing her neighbor's front door. My friend was a bit shocked and said, "Good Lord! I don't want to hurt him! What will happen?"

"Nothing," replied her madrina, "but it will scare the living crap out of him!"

A few days after my friend followed her madrina's instruction, the neighbor came over, begging forgiveness and swearing up and down that he was experiencing the worst couple days of his life.

People who do not believe in the power of magick to affect the world, yet are faced with the reports of anthropologists who observe that curses often do seem to work, try to explain it away as power of suggestion. The claim is that it's a self-fulfilling prophecy: if you know that someone has cursed you, as in the case of the Santera, your mind will react in such a way that will fulfill the curse. There is some truth to this: suggestion is a powerful thing, and if you can convince someone that they are under attack, they can manifest powerful symptoms. In fact, I have found that when people are very publicly and verbally cursed, there is rarely any ritual or spell to back it up. The reason for this isn't that curses don't work, however; it's that if someone really wants to launch a genuine magickal attack against you, they won't tip you off about it.

Most magickal and psychic attacks manifest mental symptoms in their targets. I mentioned previously the feeling of being "out of step with time" as being a precursor to crossed conditions. There are other, more serious mental symptoms that can arise as well. Some attacks, such as telepathic or hypnotic attacks, may have only mental effects. Coercive attacks that aren't geared at causing harm, but rather at getting you to do or not do certain things against your better judgment, also have primarily mental effects. The fact that the symptoms are mental does not mean that they are any less dangerous or magickal.

By far the most common mental symptoms are feelings of despair, oppression, anxiety, and fear without any identifiable cause. Inexplicable confusion or moments where you cannot focus are common. Troubled dreams are also a sign of attack.

In some cases where a spirit or artificial elemental is the agent of the attack, the target may feel that he is constantly being followed. He may hear voices when alone, see shadows and outlines of things that aren't there, and even smell scents that have no source. Smell is one of my strongest psychic areas, and I sometimes smell a hint of sulfur or rot as a first indicator of attack. Although I list this as a mental symptom because there is no physical basis for the sensation, that doesn't mean that the sights, sounds, and smells don't seem as real as anything else. Indeed, those with the ability to see may perceive much more than just the outlines and impressions of spirits!

In cases where coercive magick is being used to influence your actions, through hypnosis, telepathic control, or a spell, you may experience uncharacteristic compulsions, affinities, or aversions to things that you never did before. It is very difficult to notice this on your own because the mind tends to justify these feelings as natural, but if friends and loved ones are saying that you are acting out of character, then you should at least take a few moments and consider what they have to say. There is an old example of the hypnotist who plants the suggestion in a subject to take off his shirt or jump into the lake when he hears a certain command. After doing so, the target always explains that it was hot and really it isn't such a strange thing to do. It is only after the hypnotist plays the tape of the suggestion being planted that the subject thinks he even did anything strange! The mind is amazing at making even the strangest things seem normal.

Because all of our actions are, by and large, influenced to one extent or another by outside factors, there is a fine line between what constitutes regular influence, reasonable magickal influence, and a psychic attack. A good analogy that Dion Fortune[2] makes is that normal influence is akin to someone ringing a doorbell by pressing the button from the outside, and an attack is like lifting up the floorboards and pulling the bell wires themselves.

Stepping aside from the occult for just a moment, companies and salespeople are now making use of very advanced coercive techniques such as subliminal messages and neurolinguistic programming to influence your will. Some of this is fair, but in my opinion some of it amounts to as much of an attack as if they had done sorcery against you. Indeed, if you think that this isn't a type of sorcery, then you should take another look. The techniques that this book will teach to defend against psychic intrusion can also help avert the aggressive techniques used in sales and advertising as well.

Many of the mental signs of attack listed previously are also symptoms of mental neurosis. I want to make it very clear that people struggling with depression, schizophrenia, anxiety, ADD, or any other psychological problem should NOT substitute the magickal defenses in this book for regular therapy and psychological treatment. The degree to which the occult overlaps into conventional psychology is an interesting topic, but one beyond the scope of this book and beyond my expertise. There will likely not be any harm in using the methods in this book *alongside* of conventional treatments, but under no circumstances should they replace medical treatment.

Physical Conditions

There can also be physical symptoms associated with an attack. Headaches are a common early warning. Headaches where the scalp feels stretched too thin over the skull are particularly indicative of an attack. Sometimes when we lie down to sleep, these aches will gather to one side of the head, indicating the direction from which the attack is coming.

After headaches, fatigue would be the next most common indication. This is particularly true in cases of parasitic and vampiric attacks. In parasitic cases, someone of weak constitution and energy psychically drains someone who possesses higher vitality. This is most often unintentional and occurs commonly between family members or close friends, particularly when one is in the position of caring for the other, thus giving rise to the old adage that "the caregiver goes first."

In actual vampiric attacks, the attack is usually intentional, and there exists a whole corpus of occult teachings on vampiric magick. The first type of vampire is a living person who draws vitality from other people, willing or not, and adds that to their own power. Nowadays, this has become something of a countercultural lifestyle choice, and one can find many books on how to practice vampirism.

The second type is a bit closer to the vampire of legend in that physical death has occurred but, through special means, the person has managed to fight off the astral decay, or "second death," and sustain his etheric form by feeding on living people. When I was traveling through Budapest I was told about Magyar sorcerers who specialized in this type of magick. They would attach their spirits to living people and remain dormant during the day, but at night they would leave the host in an etheric or quasi-physical form and feed. I have never seen them, but according to the literature, you can actually spot small, almost microscopic wounds where the vampire attacks.

Fatigue is also common in cases where the target has been handed over to the dead. This is famous in Haitian vodou where it is called an "Expedition Mort." There are many ways to do it, but typically something of yours is placed in the grave of a spirit willing to do the work, and an element from that grave, usually dirt, is planted on you or your home. The idea being that you have entered the sphere of the dead, and the dead have entered the sphere of the living. This first manifests a terrible fatigue, which eventually leads to an overall breakdown. You find that you cannot stay awake, even though you have had a full night's sleep. When you are in bed, your sleep is so troubled that you get no rest. Left without treatment, the curse could lead to death.

When spirits are used in an attack, or when they are themselves on the attack as in a haunting, the most common complaint I have heard is of a weight on the chest when sleeping. This is sometimes called "Hag Riding" and occurs so commonly that there has recently been a study of the phenomenon by a professor at the University of Pennsylvania.[3] Sometimes feelings of sexual aggression accompany this sensation. It is also not unheard of to develop bruises from being attacked during the night. I have witnessed these bruises arise without physical cause when keeping vigil over a friend one night about ten years ago.

A sudden but persistent illness can also be the result of an attack. From a sudden but simple flu, to serious cancer, to completely undiagnosable illnesses, curses have the power to affect the physical shell directly. In all these cases medical attention should be sought, if only to treat the symptom while your occult defense treats the cause. In very potent attacks by powerful forces, medical events such as heart attacks and aneurysms can be the result of psychic attack, but these instances are exceedingly rare.

Loss of sexual interest and impotency can be the result of a jinx by a jealous or jilted lover. Spells for taking away "sexual nature" exist in almost all types of folk magick around the world, as do methods of restoring that nature.

Stopped-up bowels are also a favorite form of attack as evidenced in such spellbooks as Albertus Magnus's *Egyptian Secrets*[4] and the Icelandic *Galdrabok*. In fact, when I was just starting to learn rootworking in my teens, something was stolen from me and I announced generally that whoever stole it would be cursed in a most unpleasant way. Perhaps it was wrong of me, but I gathered an appropriate link to the person I suspected stole from me, and I used an old hoodoo ritual to stop up his bowels. The item was returned shortly thereafter, and I was told by a mutual friend that the spell had achieved its desired intent.

Omens and Warnings

Apart from the actual symptoms of an attack, there are omens to watch for, first among them being dreams. The oneiric realm is where our deep mind tries to communicate with the rest of the self. I will say right here that I put absolutely no stock in dictionaries of dream symbolism; each of us has our own peculiar symbol set that the deep mind makes use of in dreams. A serpent in one man's dreams will indicate danger, but to an Ophidian sorcerer like myself, it would be an excellent omen indeed. Rather than a list of symbols to watch for, I recommend looking at the overall content and character. Were you being persecuted? Pursued? Were loved ones turning their backs on you? Did you feel trapped? These are all dreams that might indicate that you were under attack. When I was suffering from the unintentional attack that I spoke of earlier, I had a strange dream that I was naked in the witness chair in a court where the judge was Rush Limbaugh. Silly as this was, the dream gave me the shivers and was one large indication that I was under attack. If you feel that you are or may be under attack, watch your dreams. If you are talented at oneiric magick, you can sometimes divine the name of the culprit from the dream itself.

Watching animals is another sign. How do they react to you? Are you finding yourself encountering more chthonic creatures such as spiders or snakes? Has anything died in your yard? Years ago, while working on behalf of a client who was under attack, a hawk died and landed right in the area where I held my circles in the yard. These and other strange occurrences should all be looked for in cases of suspected attack.

There are ways that a sorcerer can set up early warning systems to alert himself of an attack before it gets very serious. The first and easiest method is to have a plant or two in each room of the house. If you are under magickal attack, it is almost a guarantee that the plants will suffer first. For this reason, many witches keep live plants all over the house.

A classic warning of attack is to keep some silver in your shoe and around your neck. Silver dimes with holes drilled through them are famous for this in the southern United States. It is said that if you are under attack, the silver will turn black. This belief actually has some root in science, as most types of curse powders and materials such as Goofer Dust make use of sulphur, which turns silver to black.

Keeping a fresh egg on the altar can not only help indicate an attack, but also absorb some of it as well. Like the plants, an egg will take the hit of negative energy for you and go bad quickly or even break in the event of an attack.

You should also keep an eye on your amulets. When protective amulets break or get lost, it is a sign that their protection has been breeched. I always hang a Moroccan blue glass hamsa amulet to protect against the evil eye from my rearview mirror. A few days before I started getting those traffic tickets that I mentioned earlier in the chapter, the amulet broke. I didn't think anything of it at the time, but if I had been quick with a reading I might have avoided getting those tickets. Thai penis amulets that guard against impotence and are worn on a cord around the waist are another example of this. If the cord breaks, it is a sign of attack.

This collection of symptoms is by no means exhaustive. There is an endless variety of attacks that can be launched and just as many symptoms that can occur. What is important to realize is that, taken individually, everything that happens may have a logical "real world" explanation. When many of these symptoms and events all occur within a short time, however, it is a good indicator of a genuine attack. Remember to err on the side of caution, and do not ignore the symptoms when they occur.

NEW EDITION COMMENTARY

Looking at this chapter sixteen years later I think it holds up quite well. There is nothing in it that I would remove and not a whole lot to add. Just keep the following points in mind:

Anyone looking to diagnose magickal or psychic attack in someone who is experiencing mental instability is faced with a serious dilemma. On the one hand, mental instability and illness can be legitimate symptoms of a real psychic or magickal attack. On the other hand, mental instability and illness can cause people to think they are under psychic or magickal attack even when they aren't. How do you thread this needle?

My advice: Don't.

First, even if the source of the issue is psychic attack, chances are that the afflicted person still will require medical attention for the damage done, mental help included. Work with mental health professionals when appropriate; otherwise you may be feeding into someone's delusion rather than clearing it up. If you do not have access to such professionals, then you have no business treating people who are manifesting symptoms of mental illness.

Sometimes, you will run into situations where you detect no magickal attack at all, but the person seeking help insists that there is and will cite the readings of other people as proof. My advice is to simply say, "I don't detect it, so I can't diagnose it or treat it." They may walk away with the only honest answer they have gotten, or they may walk away thinking you suck at magick because everyone else assures them they are cursed. Either way, you are being honest and leaving no room to argue the point further.

The last thing I want to do is remind you that magickal attacks manifest a constellation of symptoms, not just one. If you lose your job, it doesn't mean that you are cursed. If you get sick, it doesn't mean that you are under attack. Look at others around you and see if what you are going through is unusual. If so, then look at all the categories of symptoms listed in this chapter before jumping to the idea that you are cursed.

Chapter 2

DAILY PRACTICES

Serious practitioners of magick do magick every day. Not spell work necessarily, but something that clears the mind, fortifies the spirit, and gives some protection against assaulting forces. Before we concern ourselves with defending against specific attacks, we should first develop a regimen of regular practice that will strengthen our natural defenses so that minor assaults are automatically deflected and so that we can keep ourselves grounded and centered in any more serious situation that may arise.

Just as a triangle is the most stable structure in buildings, I recommend a daily practice that covers three essential points that will assist in keeping you free and clear of psychic attack. Those three points are: meditation, banishing, and offering.

Meditation keeps the mind clear during stressful times and can, by itself, fend off many types of mental attacks. Banishing rituals clear the personal aura and free your home from negative energies and hostile spirits. Offerings serve to build a good relationship with the environment and serve as an olive branch to malevolent spirits that are attacking in retribution for human actions that upset the spiritual environment.

MEDITATION

It should be immediately apparent that one needs to keep one's head amidst any type of attack, occult or otherwise. In a magickal attack, which can cause symptoms such as paranoia, depression, and other mental distress, it becomes even more vital that you are able to control your mind and cut off these symptoms, at least long enough to launch a defense or to seek help. If I had to give up all my spiritual practices except one, I would keep meditation as that one practice. If you take only one thing away from this book and put it into practice, it should be the meditation instructions.

The word *meditation* means many things to many people. To some it is a focusing of thought on a single pressing issue, to others it is lying back and relaxing to a soothing CD, to others it is ecstatic prayer. All these things can technically be called meditation because the word itself has such a broad meaning. They are not, however, what I mean by meditation. For our purposes here we can define meditation as a process for alleviating the grasping at thoughts and cutting through mental distractions. This grasping and distraction is sometimes referred to as the "monkey mind." The term *monkey mind* refers to the way in which our minds tend to behave mechanistically and simply react to the push and pull of cause and effect, rather than make decisions from a position of pure consciousness and true will.

The genetics you inherit, the way you were raised, the friends you keep, what you watch on TV, what you eat and drink, your fight-or-flight reflex, the conversation you just had, and countless other factors all have sway over the generation of thoughts and reactions. Every moment, our thoughts are impacted by countless factors that have nothing to do with our real consciousness or true will. Almost every action that most people make is a mechanical response to one or more of these factors. Meditation is a way to cut through all these factors and reveal the primordial awareness that lies underneath the monkey mind and can act unchained by these causes and conditions.

For example, if you were to come home and find your living room windows broken, you would probably be upset. If, however, you won a million dollars in the lottery and then found the broken windows, you probably wouldn't be as upset because the good mood generated by winning the lottery would overwhelm the feelings of anger generated by the broken windows. Similarly, if you came home to find the broken windows after drinking a triple espresso, your reaction might be more severe than if you had drunk a chamomile tea instead. If we master meditation and cut through our ingrained patterns of grasping and aversion, we could choose how to react in this or any situation regardless of the circumstances leading up to it.

In Tibet, this pure awareness is described as being mirrorlike. If you look at a mirror that is reflecting flowers, you may have a very favorable reaction and think, "Very good! I love flowers." If the mirror is reflecting dog feces, your reaction will probably be very poor, thinking, "Yuck! Dog shit!" The point of the analogy is that none of these reflections changes the nature of the mirror. The mirror doesn't care if it reflects flowers or feces, it merely reflects. Your primordial awareness is like the mirror; the flowers and feces are like your thoughts and experiences. Our reactions to them on the surface involve all kinds of patterning, both learned and inherited, but if we can cut through this and rest in primordial awareness, we cut through our patterns and can act as we will, rather than as we are programmed to.

There are many types of meditation and it is a topic worth studying in depth, but as this is a book specifically about magickal defense, we should detail only a single type of meditation focused on the breath. The breath itself is said to be a mantra that everyone says 26,000 times a day. It requires no special equipment, no outward sign that you are meditating at all, so you can do it anywhere at any time. This is important because in order to benefit from meditation you must do it every day, preferably several times a day. In a situation where you feel under psychic attack at work or in a social situation, you can meditate your way to clarity without giving any outward sign that you are doing anything out of the ordinary.

Before we meditate, we should adopt a proper posture, or *asana*. There are many asanas, and you can consult a book on yoga or meditation for their descriptions. Probably the most famous asana is the Padmasana, or full lotus. Most people, however, find this position very difficult to maintain for long, and so I recommend the Siddhasana instead, which is a sort of half lotus. There are five points to this asana: The first is accomplished by bringing in the left foot in and as close to the body as possible and then bringing the right foot in either on top of, or in front of the left leg. I also recommend a cushion under the buttocks to elevate the torso, which helps the knees rest on the ground, forming a stable tripod.

The second point, which is the most essential, is to hold the back straight. To make sure that the back is straight you should reach your hands up to the sky, then lower your arms without moving your torso. This will get the back as straight as possible. Tilting the head very slightly forward straightens out the very last bit of the spine.

The third point concerns the hands. There are several ways that you can do this, and the first is to connect the thumbs to the index fingers and lay the hands, palms up, on the knees. Another is to lay the left hand in the lap, palm up, and lay the right on top of it, palm up, then connect the thumbs. There are many other hand mudras that can be used, but all of them do the same thing: connect the energy circuits of the body (nadis) and get the energy (prana) to flow into the central channel.[1]

The fourth point is to hold the tongue just behind the top front teeth. This connects a circuit of energy that runs up the back and down the front of the body.

The fifth point concerns the eyes. You can meditate with the eyes open or closed, and you should experiment to find which is best for you. If you close the eyes completely, the advantage is that you shut out visual stimuli, but for some people this only gives their imagination a blank screen on which distracting thoughts can take shape. If you meditate with the eyes open, you may be open to more distractions, but less likely to give yourself over to fantasies during the meditation. If you do keep your eyes open, you should focus them on a point about an arm's length from you, and focus with the intensity that you would have if you were threading a needle. If you can manage to focus on empty space, that is best, but, if not, you can let your eyes settle on any spot or object.

Though all these points are traditional, and will help keep the energies of the body stable during meditation and cut down on distraction, the only really essential point is to keep the back straight. If your knees bother you, or even if you just prefer it, you can use a chair rather than sitting on the floor. Simply sit normally, with your back as straight as possible. If the chair back is straight, then you can lean against it, but the spine should be as straight as you can comfortably make it. If you are in a social situation and meditating on the fly, then you should feel free to just straighten the spine as much as possible and keep the eyes as focused as possible without drawing attention.

Whatever position you take, begin your session by taking three deep breaths and release all tension and thoughts of the past, present, and future. Breathe slowly and naturally. Allow your awareness to become consumed in the breath. Do not watch it from outside like a cat watching a mouse, but rather feel that you *are* your breath. Identify your breath as the seat of your consciousness. Flow in and flow out. Fixate the mind single-pointedly on the breath at the exclusion of all else.

The past is a memory. The future is a projection. The present disappears before it can be grasped. Dwell in the breath.

If you are like most people, you will find that distractions arise nearly instantly. Once you recognize that you have left the meditation and are distracted with a train of thought, you should simply return to the breath without chastising or criticizing yourself. In fact, you should have no expectation whatsoever about how well your meditation goes. Lust for a result is the biggest obstacle to meditation. Recognize that thoughts emanate from nothing and dissipate into nothing. Rest in the breath and in primordial awareness.

In all likelihood you will at first spend most of your meditation session doing little but being distracted, recognizing it, and returning to the breath only to be distracted again. Many of my students who find themselves in this situation claim that they can't meditate and give up. What they don't realize is that they *are* meditating. They are training their mind to recognize when it is not acting according to their will, and bringing it back from distraction. Think about how valuable that is!

After a few weeks of practice you will notice that you have more control over your mind. You will be able to focus better. You will not give into anger as easily. Over time you will learn more about yourself than you can imagine. In a situation of psychic attack, you will be able to recognize the symptoms, and cut them off at the root, simply by centering in on pure awareness.

Do not shoot for long sessions right away. Start with just ten minutes in the morning right after you get up, and ten minutes right before bed. You will never have an excuse about not being able to have the time to meditate because you can almost always steal ten minutes from sleep without it affecting you at all. These two ten-minute sessions should be tied together by lots of "meditative moments" throughout the day: a minute or so of focusing on the breath and cutting through distraction. This can be done anywhere at any time—at your desk, in a restaurant, or on the toilet are all acceptable places. If you practice in this way, you will definitely see a difference in your life in a relatively short period of time.

BANISHING RITUALS

Banishing rituals are short daily rituals for grounding and centering, connecting with the divine, defining sacred space, and clearing away discursive spirits and forces. The most famous example is a ritual taught by the Hermetic Order of the Golden Dawn called the Lesser Banishing Ritual of the Pentagram (LBRP). In that order, the LBRP was considered so important you would do this ritual at least once a day for a year before learning anything further. Other similar rites include Aleister Crowley's Star Ruby and the Aurum Solis's Rousing of the Citadels. In Tibet there are many formulas for making a semskhor, or "mind circle," to accomplish the same thing. Time spent researching and experimenting with these different rituals will not be wasted.

The following ritual, the Sphere of Hekas, is a fairly simple banishing designed by me and based upon material derived from my contact with the Goddess Hekate. Rituals involving her will appear throughout the book and make a sort of Hekatean arcana in and of themselves.[2] I am not making any claims to this ritual being more effective than any other, and I invite the reader to learn several banishing rites so you can choose the one that is right for you.

THE SPHERE OF HEKAS

Part 1: Conjuring the Column

Begin by standing and facing east. Imagine that you are at the very center of the universe. I don't mean to imagine that you have left your room and are now somewhere out in space, but rather that the very place that you stand is the center of the entire universe. Just as from our perspective here on Earth it seems that the Sun revolves around us, but from a larger perspective it is revealed that the Earth revolves around the Sun, you should consider that from an even larger perspective, you are at the very center of the universe and the whole thing revolves around you.

Take a deep inhalation and imagine that above you, emanating from the highest heavens, descends a column of pure white light. This light enters the crown of your head and passes through you, down into the ground. This white light has the qualities of purification and centering. Exhale and intone the following:

DECENDAT COLUMBA!
(The descent of the dove!)

Take another deep inhalation and imagine that a reddish-colored light from beneath you rises through the column and passes through you upwards. Whereas the white light was purifying, this light is vitalizing. Exhale and intone the following:

ASCENDAT SERPENS!
(The ascent of the serpent!)

Inhale again and feel the two energies entering into you from above and below. Exhale and feel the two energies flow throughout

PROTECTION & REVERSAL MAGICK

your body, impregnating every cell of your being with their power. Feel your connection between Earth and sky, underworld and heavens.

With your right hand, point at your third eye and intone: I (ee).

Move your right hand over your heart and open your hand so that your palm faces your chest and intone: A (ah).

Move your hand lower over your genitals and turn the palm upwards, connecting the thumb and forefinger. Intone: O (oh).

This portion of the rite grounds, centers, purifies, and empowers you so that you are in a proper position to exercise authority over the forces that you wish to banish. The Dove and the Serpent are universal symbols of chthonic and ouranic forces. By conjuring the column you take in the totality of all that is, above and below. As the Magus Aleister Crowley once noted, "Adepts stand with their heads above the highest heavens and their feet below the lowest hells."[3]

After the column, you invoke the divine by the ancient formula of IAO.[4] This formula is sometimes said to be a Greek way of saying YHVH (Yahweh or Jehovah), but in reality is much older than that. In Greek, the seven vowels all equate to planets. In this case, I = the Earth, A = the moon, and O (Ω)Saturn; thus, IAO represents the whole spectrum of spheres (moon through Saturn) ruled by the Helios, the Sun. It can also be seen as an abbreviation of all the vowel sounds strung together—a powerful shamanic formula representing totality of the universe.[5]

Part 2: Delineating the Boundaries

Still standing within the column, pronounce to the powers that be:

HEKAS HEKAS ESTE BEBELOI!
(Away, away, all ye profane!)

Make a fist with your left hand and place it against your chest over your heart, cover it with your right hand and apply about five pounds of pressure there, and imagine that the force that you summoned forth from the column begins to concentrate at the heart. Imagine that this power, drawn by the physical pressure and force of will, takes the shape of a gray sphere about the size of a baseball. Visualize this until you have it very clear in your mind.

Release the pressure, and in one motion step forward with your left foot and throw your arms outward in what is called the Sign of the Enterer. As you make this sign, see the sphere at your heart grow. As it grows and spreads, it pushes back all malefic forces and harmful spirits. It grows past your body and continues until it stops where you wish to make the boundary, forming a wall of grayish astral force. Intone:

GYRUM CARPO!
(I seize the circle!)

Take your wand or athame in your hand, and extend your arm straight out. The tip of the tool (or your finger, when working without tools) should touch the edge of the circle that you want to make. If you have extended the circle past the walls of the room that you are in, then you can simply point towards the edge. Pivot, or walk the edge of your circle and intone the following:

CONSECRO ET BENEDICO ISTUM CIRCULUM
UT SIT MIHI ET OMNIBUS SCUTUM AT
PROTECTIE DEI FORTISSIMI HEKATE INVICIBILE
(I consecrate and bless this circle
That it may be to me and all a shield
And protection in the name of the most powerful invincible
    goddess Hekate)

Consider that this sphere is an invisible and impenetrable fortress surrounding you, keeping out all harmful forces and spirits of ill intent.

Part 3: Invoking the Guardians

The last section of the ritual invokes four guardians to the four corners of our sphere. Before I give the instructions for this section of the rite, I want to say a word about these particular guardians. The guardians invoked in this ritual are spirits that were revealed to me by Hekate directly and are bound by her as protective spirits. Their names are Abaek, Pyrhum, Ermiti, and Dimulgali. They have been called upon successfully by myself and the small circle of sorcerers whom I have shared this ritual with, and have proven to be powerful protectors. They can, however, be replaced with quarter guardians of your choice, such as the four Judeo-Christian archangels—Raphael, Michael, Gabriel, and Uriel—or perhaps the spirits of the four winds—Notus, Zephyrus, Boreas, and Eurus. Sets of quadruple guardians are very prevalent throughout the world.

Face east and visualize Abaek standing at the eastern edge of the circle facing the center. He has the body of a man and the head of a bull that is snorting and breathing wildly. In his hands he holds two scimitars, which he clashes together in a threatening manner. Make a gesture of conjuring and invoke:

ORKIZO ABAEK!
Bull-headed guardian of the East
Remember your vow and fill the throne
which has been set for you!

Consider that the throne (your visualization) has been filled by Abaek, and see him now turn around to face the outside of the circle.

Face south and visualize Pyrhum standing at the southern edge of the circle facing the center. He has the body of a man and the head of a horse that is breathing fire. His two hands hold a large ebony trident. Make a gesture of conjuring and invoke:

ORKIZO PYRHUM!
Horse-headed guardian of the South
Remember your vow and fill the throne
which has been set for you!

Consider that the throne (your visualization) has been filled by Pyrhum, and see him now turn around to face the outside of the circle.

Face west and visualize Ermiti standing at the western edge of the circle facing the center. She has the torso of a woman and the head and lower body of a serpent. Her hands hold a net and a skullcup, which overflows with boiling blood. Make a gesture of conjuring and invoke:

ORKIZO ERMITI!
Serpentine guardian of the West
Remember your vow and fill the throne
which has been set for you!

Consider that the throne (your visualization) has been filled by Ermiti, and see her now turn around to face the outside of the circle.

Face north and visualize Dimgali standing at the northern edge of the circle facing the center. She has the torso of a woman and the head of a black dog. In her left hand she holds a whip and in her right she holds adamantine shackles. Make a gesture of conjuring and invoke:

ORKIZO DIMGALI!
Bitch-headed guardian of the North
Remember your vow and fill the throne
which has been set for you!

Consider that the throne (your visualization) has been filled by Dimgali, and see her now turn around to face the outside of the circle.

Part 4: Closing

You have grounded and centered yourself and connected with the Earth and the heavens. You have swept away obstructing energies from your area and created a psychic barrier around you. You have invoked guardian spirits in the four directions; all that remains is to close the rite.

Take a single deep breath and bring your hands together in front of your heart as if you are praying.

PROCUL HINC PROCUL ITE PROFANI
PER NOMINA DEI ATISSIMI HEKATE
(Away, away, all ye profane
In the name of the most powerful HEKATE)

The wording of this rite is not all that important. I have used some Latin because it is one of the magickal languages and can give the ritual a feel that English may not, but if for some reason you are not comfortable with it, the general form of the rite can be followed using the English translation or some other appropriate words of similar meaning.

The ritual instructions may seem long, but once memorized the whole rite takes about five minutes to perform. Whatever banishing you choose, it should be done every day—preferably twice a day as the effectiveness of rites such as this tends to last through either sunset or sunrise.

OFFERINGS

The last point of the triad of daily practice is the making of offerings. Whereas the banishing ritual seeks to keep danger at bay by force, offerings are a pacifying practice that protects by offering an olive branch to hostile spirits and elemental forces. As stated before, the way in which we humans live can sometimes have a negative impact on the spiritual dimension, causing local guardians and forces to act against us in retribution. A large part of the shaman's role in traditional cultures deals with mending these harmful breaches and smoothing out the relationship between this world and the next. By making offerings we are sending a signal to those forces that any breaches such as building or trampling on power spots and polluting the air and water were accidental and that we are attempting to make reparations.

Apart from the value that offerings have in deterring crossed conditions and attacks, they are a potent means of gaining spiritual allies and aiding your sorcery to manifest materially. If you establish a regular practice of making offerings to the powers that be, you will find the universe all too willing to aid you in your witchcraft because of the bonds you have formed through the power of offering.

As to what is offered, there are many types of offerings that can be made, both physical and emanated from the mind. I do not mean to undercut the importance of physical offerings, but the first thing that one finds after making a physical offering to the spirits is that in a few hours, the stuff is still there physically. Though it is said that some rare and powerful spirits can manifest physically and devour their offerings, most beings feed upon the subtle essence of the physical offerings rather than the substance itself. The exception to this is burnt substances of fumigation. There are many spirits who can take nourishment directly from the smoke produced by burnt herbs, plants, and woods. Even if you use solid physical offerings such as cakes and alcohol, you can increase the power of the offering by mentally multiplying these offerings through force of will and seeing them fill infinite space.

Offerings need not always be done ceremoniously or formally. You can leave a dime or some whiskey on a grave, lay some flowers or pour some water near a tree or plant, or burn some incense in the backyard and mentally offer it to the ten directions. Acts of generosity like this, no matter how small, serve to build up a good relationship with the spiritual forces around your home and wherever you travel.

If you do want to make a formal ritual offering, the following is a ritual that is short enough to be done regularly, if not daily. The rite rewards protectors and familiars who have worked on your behalf and pacifies those spirits that would cause obstacles and harm to you and those under your protection. This rite speaks to elemental and spirit forces generally. The potential to make this a more elaborate offering ritual geared at specific classes of spirits exists, but care should be taken as to what is offered. Certain spirits can be offended if the wrong type of offering is made. For instance, in some Afro-Caribbean traditions an offering of salt will upset the dead, and in the Himalayas offerings of meat will enrage the Nagas. In the future I hope to publish a more detailed book on the classes of spirits and offerings traditional to each. In the meantime, if you want to make more elaborate offerings to specific types of beings, let research, omens, and dreams guide you in your efforts.

In the following rite, the physical support for the offerings will be some incense or a burnt wood such as juniper or sandalwood.

If you are doing the rite outside, you can add to this some water, tea, or whiskey to spill on the ground as a libation. Because you are making offerings to spirits that may initially be hostile to you, I recommend staying away from herbs that aid in the manifestation of spirits such as dittany of Crete or mullein. I call the incense a "physical support" because you will be feeding that incense with energy directly, visualizing it filling all space, and willing it to take on whatever shape is most pleasing to the recipient.

Take your incense and your libation, if you have one, and arrange them on an altar or table. Don't light the incense yet.

Part 1: Purification of the Offerings

Hold your hands over the offerings forming the triangle of manifestation between your hands. Say the following:

> By Earth, the body of the gods
> By Water, their flowing blood
> By Air, the breath of the gods
> By Fire, their burning soul

> May these offerings be made blessed and made pure.

As you say this, consider that any impurities in the offerings are washed, blown, and burned away.

Part 2: Inviting the Guests

IO EVOHE! IO DAEMONES! DAIMONES EVOHE!
Spirits of the firmament of Earth and of ether
Spirits of the dry land and of the flowing water
Spirits of the whirling air and of rushing fire

Come! Come!
Phantoms of the dead, the quick, and in-between
To those to whom I owe debt and who owe debt unto me
Famulus and guardians who are bound unto me!
Come! Come!
Every dryad, sylph, and satyr who dwells within this place
Every undine and salamander, every fey and gnomish spirit!
Every succubi and incubi, every spectre of ill will
Come! Come!
All spirits who cause help or harm in response to human
    action!
Come here according to your desires, be seated on the
    thrones
Io Evohe! Come! Come!

Part 3: Making the Offering

Light the incense. Give the sign of offering, which is done by rubbing your palms together several times until they become hot. Then turn your palms upward, and, as the heat leaves your hands, imagine that clouds of offerings flow from them and mingle with the incense smoke, filling all space.

Clouds of offerings, I give to you
Food and drink and fumigation
Enjoy! Enjoy!
Let the offerings arise and pervade all space
Let it take the form that is most desired
Enjoy! Enjoy!
Friends and family from former lives
I am grateful for your past kindness

Enjoy! Enjoy!
You who form obstacles as retribution to my action
Forgive any offense made by mistake or delusion
Enjoy! Enjoy!
Spirits of the dead and trapped in-between spaces
Wardens of this ground and keepers of the winds
Enjoy! Enjoy!
Guardians and familiars, be thou fulfilled
Quickly realize my hopes and desires
Enjoy! Enjoy!
To each of you I offer inexhaustible treasures and
Delightful substances and enjoyments.
You who would harm me
Partake of this feast and be at peace
You who would help me
Be fulfilled and accomplish that with which you
        are charged

After making this charge, you can either go directly on to the next section, or sit and try to commune with the forces invoked.

Part 4: License to Depart

Honored guests of this temple, the window of our commu-
        nion is closing,
Take your last taste of these enjoyments and go in peace.
Vacate the thrones of the feast and go forth unto your
        abodes and habitations as you desire,
Forever act as friends and helpers.
So Mote It Be

These three practices of meditation, banishing, and offering should all become regular parts of your magickal regimen. The ideal would be to do all three every day, meditation and banishings perhaps twice a day. This seems like a lot, but really it isn't much time at all, especially after you learn the rituals by heart. If you cannot do them or similar practices daily, then you should at least shoot to meditate and banish three or four times a week and perform offerings at least once a week.

NEW EDITION COMMENTARY

It's rare I make a sweeping change of policy, but I must do it for this chapter. I no longer recommend daily banishings be part of your regular practice. It's not that they are harmful; I did them for decades and benefitted from them. From the perspective of safety and protection it's a good practice. Too good, in fact.

You don't wear a full set of head-to-toe battle armor every time you leave the house, do you? Of course not. Even police officers don't wear full tactical gear when they are on patrol. It would be great protection but would make other things like walking, shopping, or having a friendly conversation difficult.

If you are a witch, magician, or sorcerer of any kind, you are probably trying to make connections with spirits, not keep them at bay all the time.

The traditions that suggest banishings like the LBRP every day try to get the magician as existing in a perfectly controlled space that allows in only those spirits that they choose to let in. I don't care for this view of magick and don't think it's even possible. Just like I wouldn't choose to live my life in a plastic bubble, I don't think it's advisable or necessary to banish daily. You might find that forging relationships with local spirits provides even better protection than any sphere or shield.

So why is it still in the chapter? Because if you suspect you are under magickal attack, or are undertaking something particularly dangerous, daily banishings are a **very** good idea. That is precisely the time you should be putting on that battle armor. The Sphere of Hekas has proven an excellent aid to those who need it. The question at hand is: Do you need it all the time?

Instead of a tripod of meditation, offerings, and banishings, you would probably be better served by meditation, offerings, and devotion. This doesn't have to be very religious or prayerful. There are yogas, mantras, and energetic practices that would fit the bill. What you will get from these daily practices over time is a resonance with the powers you choose and an ability to mediate their powers into the world. You will work to connect with these powers, and they will notice you in turn, whether they are gods and goddesses or local spirits of the land.

Strong relationships and resonance with spirits are a more enduring type of protection than even banishing and shields. I have included a daily devotional prayer and chant to Hekate as an appendix to this new edition.

Chapter 3

PERSONAL PROTECTION

After establishing a regular regimen of meditation, offering, and banishing you will find yourself much more grounded, clear, and aware than you were previously. Most attacks and intrusions against your peace will roll right off of you. There will, however, be times when you need to address a situation directly and with stronger force than just your regular banishing rituals. You may also find yourself in the position of helping a nonpractitioner who has no regular spiritual practice to clear away crossed conditions and attacks, in which case you will need to employ some of the specific protection rituals that follow.

SHIELDS

During times of crossed conditions and psychic distress it is vital that you be extra-diligent with the regular meditations, offerings, and banishings that were taught in the previous chapter. You may also want to supplement them with an additional layer of protection, which is where the shield comes in.

Shields require no equipment other than your own will and imagination, and thus are the first line of defense when you feel attacked. Shields can be helpful not only against occult dangers, but also in psychological attacks from annoying coworkers, overzealous salespeople, brutal bosses, and any other disgruntled people whom you may encounter. Shields are also an excellent way of protecting yourself from negative influences that may be present in a place, without actually banishing those influences. This may be desirable if you find yourself in certain power spots with hostile guardians or in a house where very negative people live.

A shield is created in a manner similar to how you conjure the sphere in the banishing ritual from Chapter 2.

Begin by calling to mind the column of energy connecting you to the heavens and to the Earth. As this is more of a psychic technique than a ritual, there is no need for words; simply see the column descend from the heavens passing through you down into the Earth, and feel the vital current arise from the Earth into you.

As you inhale, feel the power from above and below flow into you. As you exhale, feel that energy move throughout your body, impregnating every cell of your body with power. Make a fist with your left hand and place it over your heart. Cover it with your right hand and apply about five pounds of pressure. As you inhale, feel the power gather at your heart, attracted there by the pressure and your focused will. See a small, gray egg shape gather at your heart. Release the pressure on your chest and feel the egg grow larger, passing through your skin and stopping just at the point where it is roughly one to two feet away from your physical body. Imagine that the surface of this egg is impenetrable, and that all malign forces will be unable to break its barriers.

After the image has been strongly conjured in the mind and you *know* that the shield is there, simply turn your attention away from it and go about your business. In general, the effects of the shield will wear off in a few hours unless continually fed with imagination and will. If you desire to dissolve the shield before then, simply inhale deeply, then exhale and see the shield dissolve into space.

There are several variants on this technique and ways to alter the shield to create different effects. For instance, in some cases rather than protect directly, it may be desirable to confuse or throw your enemies off-kilter. In this case, make the shield the same way but instead of seeing the shield as gray, visualize its surface as swirling colors, like when sunlight hits oil on water. I first started using this confusion shield at a job where there was one particular manager who was very verbally abusive and seemed to be something of an unconscious psychic vampire. He always seemed to walk away from his arguments with a feeling of energy, leaving his targets drained and listless. When I started employing the shield of swirling colors, he would get frustrated and start to lose track of why he was berating me in the first place. He would stumble over his words and get confused about what he wanted, and then he would storm off to his office. Eventually, he left me alone.

If you experiment with different visualizations and energetic keys, you will find many different ways in which you can alter the effect of your shield. For instance, you can make shields corresponding to the four elements. To do this, rather than drawing in power from the column as discussed on page 52, concentrate on the color and qualities of the element invoked. I will talk more about the elements in a later chapter, but in the meantime you can use the following correspondences.

Element	Color	Qualities
Fire	Red	Hot, Dry, and Expansive
Water	Blue	Cool, Wet, and Fluid
Air	Yellow	Warm, Wet, and Rapid Movement
Earth	Brown	Cool, Dry, Dense, and Heavy

Concentrate on the qualities of one of these elements, and, as you inhale, *will* yourself to breathe in that element from the space around you. As you exhale, see your body filling up with the element. Then create the shield as before: Place the hand and fist over your heart and see the sphere gather there, but in the color associated with the element. Project it out into an egg around you, and see that energy forming a shell around you.

The elemental shield has many uses. Primarily it makes an excellent defense against any attacks by elementals of an opposing element (that is, Water vs. Fire, Air vs. Earth). You can also use the shield to boost certain qualities in you: Earth for grounding and centering, Air for intelligence and cunning, Water for understanding and wisdom, Fire for energy and firm will.

The reason that shields appear in this section and not in the regular practice chapter is that, whereas a banishing is patterned specifically against harmful powers, a shield works against everyone. Leaving a shield up all the time will tend to cut you off from people, and even those who mean you nothing but good may find you seem distant or unapproachable. Using confusion or elemental shields can cause even stranger reactions. Use them only when you feel that you need them.

INVISIBILITY

There are some situations where the best protection is obfuscation rather than confrontation. It may be that you want to withdraw from the chaos of the world for a bit in order to sort out your next move or that you want not to be noticed while you are laying down your own reversal or counter-magick.[1] Whatever the reason, magickal invisibility can offer a type of protection that banishing rituals do no not.

To be clear, this ritual will not actually make you transparent, nor will it make light bend around you or in any way allow you to walk around naked amazing people with a disembodied voice and objects that float in space. Magickal invisibility conceals your aura and causes people who are not specifically looking for you to not notice you. If someone is looking for you and he bumps into you in the hallway, he will see you just fine, though he may comment on there being something different about you that day. You may also find that those people whom you do interact with forget those interactions afterward.

As an example, when I first started experimenting with magickal invisibility in college, I was passed over time and time again when offering comments in class, though previously I seemed to be one of the professor's favorite students to pick on. Later, when I had a falling out with some friends I was living with, I used the same invisibility rituals and was promptly left alone, even to the point of one of them talking about me while I was in the room because he forgot I was there.

As with the shields, you must be careful about when you employ invisibility. I was once in a fender bender that could have been much worse because someone pulled out of a parking lot without seeing my car. The person apologized profusely and swore up and down that he had looked, he just didn't see me.

Of course the reason that invisibility is included in this book isn't to be able to merely avoid uncomfortable situations, but for protection. In the case of a magickal attack, particularly one where spirits are employed against you, using invisibility as a defense will have the effect of giving the hostile spirit no one to attack. Eventually, the spirit will return to where it came from. If it was sent by another witch, it will carry with it the curse that was intended for you. If it was just a hostile-natured spirit of some kind, it will simply return to its own habitat.

The only tool that you will need for this ritual is some incense. If you can use myrrh (alone, with frankincense, or with dragon's blood), that is best; if not, then you can use just about any incense that you like.

The ritual begins with conjuring the column just like in the banishing ritual from the last chapter.

Part 1: Conjuring the Column

Begin by standing and facing east. Imagine that you are at the very center of the universe.

Take a deep inhalation and imagine that above you, emanating from the highest heavens, descends a column of pure white light. This light enters the crown of your head and passes through you, down into the ground. This white light has the qualities of purification and centering. Exhale and intone the following:

DESCENDAT COLUMBA!
(The descent of the dove!)

Take another deep inhalation and imagine that a reddish-colored light from beneath you rises through the column and passes through you upwards. Whereas the white light was purifying, this light is vitalizing. Exhale and intone the following:

ASCENDAT SERPENS!
(The ascent of the serpent!)

Inhale again and feel the two energies entering into you from above and below. Exhale and feel the two energies flow throughout your body, impregnating every cell of your being with their power. Feel your connection between Earth and sky, underworld and heavens.

With your right hand point at your third eye and intone: I (ee).

Move your right hand over your heart and open your hand so that your palm faces your chest and intone: A (ah).

Move your hand lower over your genitals and turn the palm upward, connecting the thumb and forefinger. Intone: O (oh). Stand for a moment and meditate on your connection to the Earth and sky, the underworld and heavens, and your connection to the divine.

Part 2: Occulting the Cross Quarters

Stand in the center of your temple (or wherever) facing east and proclaim:

Hekate, mother of night Helios, father of light
Cloak me in shadows and smoke
That I may pass unseen among men.

Take the censer or stick of incense and hold it above your head, moving it in a pattern similar to the infinity sign. Vibrate the name IAO.

Move the incense below you so that you are holding it close to the floor. Move it in the same infinity pattern. Vibrate the name OAI.

Move to the southeast and make the same pattern vibrating AOI.

Move to the southwest and make the same pattern vibrating OIA.

Move to the northwest and make the same pattern vibrating AIO.

Move to the northeast and make the same pattern vibrating IOA.

Return to the southeast, completing the circle. Then move back to the center of the temple and place the incense back in its holder.

Part 3: Splitting Space

Stand in the center of the temple again and recall the feeling that you are at the very center of the universe. Rub your hands together until they are warm, which brings the power into the hands. Keeping your palms together, move your hands forward as if you are moving them into the seam between two curtains. Indeed, you should have it in mind that you are inserting your hands *into space itself*. Once you have inserted your hands, move them apart as if you were parting the curtains—you may actually be able to feel the pressure of parted space on the backs of your hands as you part them.

Once your hands are parted, turn your right palm up and your left palm down. Start moving them again, right hand upward, left hand down—parting another of the three dimensions of space.

Face your right palm forward and your left palm backwards, and move them apart, splitting space around you. Thus you have split all three dimensions of space—width, height, and depth—around your body.

Place your hands at your sides. Say:
By Hekate, the mother of night
By Helios, the father of light

I stand outside of space
I go forth in silence and shadow
So shall it be.

Place your right index finger to your lips. This is called the sign of silence or the sign of Harpocrates. Inhale and imagine that your physical body is empty of tangible substance. Exhale completely and feel yourself blend seamlessly into your surroundings. Hold your breath after the exhale for as long as you comfortably can, and meditate on your removal from normal space. Go forth in silence and shadow.

CLEANSING AND PROTECTION BATHS

Spiritual baths are one of the oldest strata of magickal practice on this planet. From time immemorial, sacred baths have been believed to clean far more than just the body, and the purity of water used in conjunction with certain herbs, minerals, and oils can yield very potent results. We see evidence of sacred baths mentioned as far back as the Sumerian Hymn to Nanna, and see their practice reflected everywhere today from the Christian baptism to the health spa. All over the world are places of power dedicated to magickal bathing: Varanasi's ghats on the Ganga River, Haiti's waterfall of Saut d'Eau, and the bathing pool in King Arthur's courtyard at Glastonbury.

While some Western practitioners seem to skip bathing and purification in favor of more energy-based practices, such as the banishings and shields, the magickal bath is an important way to ground your magick onto the physical plane, achieving more tangible results. There is no better way to cleanse yourself of negative influences, and I recommend that ritual bathing always be a part of whatever plan of defense you employ against troubling forces.

The first consideration when putting together a bath ritual is the water itself. Traditionally, you would use water from a natural source such as a spring, lake, or water collected during rainstorms. If you live near a sacred spring or river, that is ideal as a source of water, but the general idea is that the more natural the source of the water, the better. That said, I will admit that most of the time I end up using tap water and suspect most of my clients do so as well. It is far better to use tap water than not to take the bath at all!

After you are settled on the water to be used, you need to know what you are adding to the bath. Formulas typically call for three or more ingredients, usually odd numbers. These ingredients can be mineral, herbal, or zoological, and what they symbolize defines the nature of the bath. There are traditional bathing formulas for everything from drawing money and love, to influencing those around you, to repelling jinxes and negativity. It is this last category that we are concerned with here, and the following are three examples of simple formulas that we can use. (Please note that these formulas are recommended for use only by adults, and everyone should be careful with sensitive areas of the skin.)

Protection

A good protection bath includes *salt, ammonia,* and *vinegar.* The salt and vinegar can be equal parts of about a half a cup or so, but the ammonia should be only a teaspoon diluted in at least four gallons of water, as it is toxic and can be harmful if inhaled. Ammonia is considered such a strong cleaner that if more is used it will remove not only negative influences, but positive and neutral ones as well.

Cleansing

White oak bark, cinnamon, and *pine needles* comprise a formula that I like for cleaning away jinxes and negativity. A hyssop bath is also traditional, especially for clearing evil that you brought upon yourself.

These ingredients can be added liberally to bathwater.

Reversing Harm

Eucalyptus leaves, red pepper, and *rue.* This is specifically for reversing harm back upon a sender and can be used in conjunction with the spells in Chapter 7. You can add approximately a half a cup each of eucalyptus leaves and rue, and a pinch of red pepper.

These three bath formulas are just a sample of the almost infinite combinations that exist amongst traditional formulas for protection and reversal.

Timing is also a factor in the bath. Most often, baths are prescribed to be taken just before dawn so that the rising Sun is working with you. If you know that you are going to confront someone who is working against you, or you are traveling to an area that is infested with a bad psychic ambience, then taking a protection bath right before that confrontation is also a good idea. If you are afflicted with your symptoms at night, then bathing before bed would be the best idea. Follow the lunar phases (waning moon for driving away and waxing for attracting) or the planetary days of the week for timing your bath. But in the cases where an attack is manifesting now, it is better to start the ball rolling immediately rather than waiting for the proper day or moon phase. Let common sense and your own inclinations be your guides.

I should mention here that the ritual bath is not a bath to get you physically clean. You are not concerned with lathering and shampooing, only with ritual. The manner in which you wash during the bath is very important: scrub up from the feet to the head to draw things to you, down from the head to the feet to push energy away from you, and soak to alleviate symptoms. During the bath there is often the reading of a spell or prayer. For instance, in hoodoo, and also in Solomonic magick, certain Psalms would be read during the bath, such as the twenty-third for protection and the fifty-first for purification. A Pagan might do well to recite one of the protection incantations from the *Papyri Graecae Magicae*. Words of your own will often do as well as or better than these traditional readings, and you should feel free to use anything that fits the situation.

Here is an incantation that calls upon Hekate and Helios, which fits well with the other rituals in this book:

Hail to you, Hekate of the threshold
Hail to you, Helios most high
Lay your hands upon me in consecration
Drive sickness and evil from my limbs.
May these waters drive away my attackers
And cast them down into the four rivers of Hades
May the air blow them away to the four winds
May I forever stand in your luminous light
And have my path made clear.
Hail to you, Hekate of the threshold
Hail to you, Helios most high.

In the old days, before indoor plumbing, people typically washed themselves in basins that they could then carry outside and dump. Another traditional element of a spiritual bath taken at dawn would be the dumping of water towards the rising Sun in the east, and thus the final casting out of any negativity drawn out during the bath. Of course, in this day and age we mostly bathe indoors, and so I understand that most people will want to use their bathtub drain to get rid of the water. I admit that I myself most often take my baths in the tub and let the water flow down the drain, but I have used a basin and done it the traditional way as well. In matters that are very important to me, I find it worthwhile to do it the old-fashioned way. Try it both ways for yourself, and see if you don't find a difference.

AMULETS, TALISMANS, AND CHARMS

Much has been made about the difference between amulets and talismans. Some, such as Donald Michael Kraig, claim that an amulet drives forces away and a talisman attracts things. Others claim that amulets refer only to those charms found in nature that are imbued with innate qualities, such as hagstones, and talismans refer to objects crafted by the witch and charged in a ritual. There doesn't seem to be much linguistic support to either of these claims, and I won't argue one way or the other. What is important is that the carrying of charms is one of the best-known and most widely practiced methods of magickal protection on the planet. Certainly this form of magick has crossed over into mainstream culture more than any of the other practices in this book, and it is not uncommon to find rabbit's feet, saint medallions, or rune necklaces worn by folks who consider themselves to be about as far from witchcraft as can be.

Amongst naturally occurring amulets, iron ranks as the king of protective substances.[2] Its use in protecting against spirits, witches, and fairies is well known all over the world. So disruptive is iron to spirits that some traditions of the craft do not allow any metal inside the circle until it is well consecrated and stable. Many old cemeteries are surrounded by iron fences with spikes not only to keep intruders out, but to keep the ghosts *in*. Before we learned to mine and smelt iron, a major source of iron for ancient man was meteorites that had a high concentration of iron and nickel. This sky-iron is particularly valued in magick and is one of the metals called for in the traditional construction of the Tibetan phurba.[3]

The practice of driving an iron nail or knife into the doorframe to keep witches out is well known throughout Europe and possibly derives from Pliny's *Historia Naturalis*, which talks of iron's apotropaic properties:

> "[F]or take a knife or dagger and make an imaginary circle two or three times with the point thereof, upon a child, or an elder body, and then go round withal about the party as often, it is a singular preservative against all poisons, sorceries, or enchantments. Also to take any iron nail out of the coffin or sepulchre wherein man or woman lieth buried, and to stick the same fast to the lintel or side post of a door, leading either into the house or bed-chamber where any doth lie who is haunted with spirits in the night, he or she shall be delivered and secured from such fantastical illusions."

Note that not only does Pliny speak of iron's ability to disrupt enchantments, but specifically of the power of an iron coffin nail. Coffin nails are particularly valued in hoodoo practice as well and are used both in the laying of curses and the protection from them. I myself have a cross made from two iron coffin nails, which serves as a powerful protective amulet.

PROTECTION & REVERSAL MAGICK

The cross itself is also a powerful protective symbol and has a history that extends much further back than Christianity. The equal-armed cross is one of the oldest religious symbols on Earth and has spawned many variants, including the crux ansata, or ankh, of Egypt; and the swastika, which is known as the yungdrung, or the eternal, in Tibet, and the fylfot, meaning four feet, in Europe. The symbolism of the cross is manifold and can indicate the meeting of two worlds or planes, the spinning wheel of the Sun, or the division of the world into the four directions. Its use as a symbol of the sacrificed god should not be overlooked and is not restricted only to the Christian tradition. The Persian/Roman Mithras, the Etruscan God Ixion, and the Aztec Quetzalcoatl have all been shown crucified on crosses of one kind or other.

You can certainly purchase a cross to wear as an amulet, but I have always found the actual binding of two beams together to be a powerful moment and an ideal time to charge the cross ritually, so I recommend making your own. The material is up to you, but it should have meaning. You can use a sacred wood such as rowan, oak, or thorn, or you could use the aforementioned iron nails (coffin nails can be difficult to come by, so you may just have to find iron nails at a hardware store), or bones. Chicken bones or other animal bones will more than suffice, but you can use human bones if you want, which can be purchased legally from places such as the Bone Room in California.[4] If you do use bones, be sure to make an offering to the spirit that is attached to the bones and do a divination to see if there will be any obstructions in using them.

To work the spell, simply hold the two beams of the cross out in front of you with your arms fully extended, in a pose similar to someone in a horror movie repelling a vampire by holding two sticks together. Visualize the arms of the cross extending outward into infinity, and focus your mind on the point where they cross. As you hold the cross out, make a proclamation such as:

By Boreas, Zephyrus, Eurus, and Notus
By Phlegethon, Cocytus, Styx, and Acheron
By all the princes and powers of the four directions
I bind and consecrate this cross
That it may forever be a shield and protection
Against all manner of malevolent powers
Hateful spirits and baleful spells.
By Will and Word
So Shall It Be!

After charging the cross, set it down upon the altar or on the ground without separating the beams, and bind them together by wrapping them in black string or leather. If you are working with iron and have the skill, you can weld the cross together.

Apart from the cross, there is an almost infinite variety of protective symbols that can be purchased or made into amulets:

• The hamsa hand, also known as the hand of Fatima (the daughter of Mohammed) or hand of Miriam (sister of Moses and Aaron), is a popular symbol of protection from the Middle East. It consists of a downward pointing hand usually with an eye in the middle.

• A variation of the hamsa hand is the eye set in blue glass, found everywhere in Morocco, Turkey, Italy, and also in Santeria. This takes numerous forms, ranging from a simple eye painted onto a small circle of blue glass, to a blue hamsa hand with an eye, to ornate horseshoes with eyes painted on them.

- The Palad Khik, or surrogate penis, of Thailand is a penis amulet usually with a monkey, tiger, or some other animal riding on top of it. The penis amulet protects against spirits and spells that would cause infertility or loss of virility and would be worn on the belt. If it falls off, that is a sign that it has done its job and absorbed an attack on behalf of your actual genitals.

- The triskele is shaped like a three-armed swastika. It is composed of three bent legs united at the thigh. In Greece and Italy it often has a Gorgon or Medusa head at the center and petrifies any witch or harmful person.

- Italy's mano fico and mano cornuto are protective hand gestures that are commonly seen on hand amulets. The mano fico, or fig hand, places the thumb in between the index and middle fingers of the closed fist. The mano cornuto, or horned hand, raises the index and pinkie fingers up from a closed fist, representing horns. Both of these amulets can be made from silver, iron, or pewter, but are especially potent when made from blood-red coral.

- The silver dime is a particularly American protective amulet. Not only does it have the protective qualities of silver, but it also is said to turn black if someone has cursed you. This belief originates in the practice of placing silver dimes in your shoes, where a root doctor would put Goofer Dust, Hot-Foot Powder, or some other cursing powder. These powders almost always have sulfur in them, which would turn the dime black.

The list of traditional protective amulets could and does fill several books, but these are a good start to any collection of apotropaic charms.

Apart from these amulets, there are talismanic seals that can be drawn on parchment or engraved on an appropriate metal. An endless variety of these can be found in grimoires such as the Keys of Solomon. The two most famous of these are the so-called "Sator Square" and the "Abracadabra" charm.

The Sator Square is derived from a Latin palindrome that reads SATOR AREPO TENET OPERA ROTAS and can be arranged into a magick square:

S	A	T	O	R
A	R	E	P	O
T	E	N	E	T
O	P	E	R	A
R	O	T	A	S

Figure 3.1 Sator Square

Sator means "to sow." *Tenet* means "to hold." *Opera* means "work, care, or effort." *Rotas* means "wheel." *Arepo* is a more troubling word, as it doesn't appear in Latin. Some think it indicates a proper name, others believe it is borrowed from Gaulish and means "to plough." Still others believe that it is an Aramaic version of the Greek phrase for Alpha and Omega. This last interpretation is supported by the fact that you can arrange the letters to form the words Pater Noster (Our Father) in a cross leaving only two As and Os left over, thus making a Christian amulet that looks like Figure 3.2 on page 69.

PROTECTION & REVERSAL MAGICK

Another anagram can be made from the square that makes the phrase Satan, ter oro te, reparato opes (Satan, I bid you thrice: Return my fortune back to me). Whatever its true meaning, it has been used since the fall of Pompeii in protective magick and continues to be used to this day. It is not uncommon to find the seal used amongst the Pennsylvania Dutch as a hex sign.

Figure 3.2 Paternoster Cross

Abracadabra is a magickal word that unfortunately has gotten a bad reputation in modern times because of its use by stage magicians to dress up their feats of prestidigitation. The word once enjoyed a reputation as an ancient word of power, and there are several versions of its origin. The most accepted etymology of the word is that it comes from the Aramaic word *avra kehdabra*, which means "I create as I speak." Another possibility is that word comes from a different Aramaic phrase: *abhadda kedhabhra* meaning "disappear like this word." It is this last meaning that lends itself best to its use as a written amulet.

The amulet is simply the word *Abracadabra* written over and over again, dropping one letter each time. The charm first appeared in the 2nd century in *De Medicina Praecepta* by Serenus Sammonicus, physician to the Roman emperor Caracalla, and is reputed to drive away disease. Since then it has been used as a magickal charm to drive away not only disease, but also malevolent spirits and curses.

ABRACADABRA
ABRACADABR
ABRACADAB
ABRACADA
ABRACAD
ABRACA
ABRAC
ABRA
ABR
AB
A

Certain herbs and minerals are carried as protective amulets as well. Salt, for instance, is said to drive away unwanted people. Asafoetida drives away disease and curses, and pretty much anything else that smells it. Devil's shoestring binds up evil spirits. Agar-agar helps make you invisible and can be used in conjunction with the invisibility ritual on pages 55–59. These, along with broom, dragon's blood, garlic, mistletoe, eucalyptus, citronella, rosemary, lemons, and mandrake, are just some of the herbs that can be carried alone or in a conjure hand.

The conjure hand is also known as a mojo bag or gris-gris bag. The word *gris-gris* means "gray-gray" and indicates that the bag has a combination of white and black magick at work in it. These bags are a staple of the American hoodoo tradition and are made for a variety of purposes.[5] Conjure hands for protection can be made by gathering the appropriate materials into a flannel drawstring bag of an appropriate color (usually red) or binding them up in cloth, as is the style in New Orleans. The number of ingredients should be an odd number—three, seven, and nine being the most common. You should avoid bags with more than thirteen ingredients.

Here are a few simple three-ingredient formulas that I like:

The Devil's Hand [6]

Nine pieces of devil's shoestring to bind up the evil, a devil nut to scare it off, and some asafoetida, which is also called devil's dung, to drive it away. Place it all in a black bag.

A Reversing Hand

Eucalyptus leaves, salt, and crab shells carried in a red bag will reverse spells and harm back upon the sender.

Angelic Protection

Particularly potent for women is a conjure hand of angelica root, balm of Gilead buds, and salt. Carry in a white cloth. This hand is said to smooth things out in a less confrontational way than a reversing or straight-on shielding charm.

Jinx Breaker

Saltpeter, sulfur, and lemongrass carried in a red flannel bag is a good formula for breaking up a jinx and opening the door to new opportunity.

Travel Protection

Mugwort, comfrey leaves, and fennel will keep you safe during travel, warding off not only harmful energies, spirits, and spells, but the law as well.

Whether you use one of these formulas, a traditional formula from somewhere else, or one of your own devising, a mojo bag should be consecrated and enlivened with spirit. A traditional American rootworker might use a psalm or an impromptu prayer to charge a bag, and you should feel free to do the same if you like. Some rootworkers talk to the bag as if it were alive, and give it instructions. In *Voodoo Tales as Told among the Negroes of the Southwest: Collected from Original Sources* the folklorist Mary Alicia Owen has made a record of one such ritual performed on a charm that she hired a root doctor named King to make for Charles Godfrey Leland, the author of *Aradia, or the Gospel of the Witches.*

> "Now," said he, addressing the ball, as he dangled it between his thumb and finger, "yo' name is Leland, Charles Leland. Ise gwine ter sen' yo' er long way off unter er master, er mighty long way off, 'cross big watteh (the ocean). Go out in de woods an' 'fresh yo'se'f 'fo' yo' staht. Go 'long! Do yo' hyeah me? Is yo' gwine? Is yo' gwine way off? Is yo' climbin'? Is yo' climbin' high?"
>
> After each question there was a series of answerings, growing fainter and fainter as the spirit of the ball was supposed to go farther and farther away.[7]

You can do something completely spontaneous, compose your own charge to the bag, or use a spell from whatever tradition you come from. As I hold the serpent sacred as an agent of gnosis and magick, I often use a Greek chant I call the Serpent's Song to charge a bag while holding it over an appropriate incense or the smoke from a candle flame.

HO OPHIS HO ARCHAIOS
HO DRAKON HO MEGAS
HO EN KAI, HO ON KAI
HO ZON TOUS AIONAS
META TOU PNEUMATOS SOU!
(Oh, Ancient Serpent
Oh, Great Dragon
Who was and who is
Throughout the Aeions
Be thou with our spirit.)

When I sing this, a sufficient number of times, I usually feel a change in the air, as if several invisible doors are opening around me, or there is a sudden shift in awareness, as if I can't remember for a moment how I got there. Once I am done, I spit into the bag and say: SO SHALL IT BE.

The Wheel of Hekate
In keeping with the Hekatean spells in this book, I want to present a seal and charge that appeared to me in a dream after a Hekate working in 2002. The symbol is simple enough and looks like a wheel of tridents or pitchforks.

Figure 3.3

It can be inscribed on parchment or engraved in metal. It can also be painted on the floor as a magickal circle of protection. The charge of the symbol invokes not only Hekate, but four groups of the triple feminine figures from Greek mythology: the Furies, the Graces, the Fates, and the Gorgons. To charge the seal, hold your hands in the gesture called the Triangle of Manifestation (palms facing the seal, tips of the thumbs and index fingers together making a triangle through which you can view the object that you are charging). Use the following invocation to charge the seal:

Hail to Hekate, keyholder of the world
Hail to Enodia, keeper of the triple road
Hail to Nekuia, guardian of the grave
Nether, Nocturnal, and Inferal one
I call thee by thy three secret names
Ereshkigal, Nebotosoaleth, Aktiophis.
Oh, Hekate!
By your name I call forth the fates!
All powerful Morae
Clotho, Lachesis, and Atropos
I stir, conjure, and call thee!
You, who originate, measure, and cut the fabric of life
Take mercy upon thy thread
And spin the tide of battle in my favor
Oh, Hekate!
By your name I call forth the furies!
Terrible ones spawned from the blood of Uranus
Alecto, Tisiphone, Megaera
I stir, conjure, and call thee!
Come forth from Erebus and protect the bearer of this seal
Through righteous wrath drive out all attackers!

May not even the names of my enemies exist!
Oh, Hekate!
In your name I call forth the Gorgons!
Serpent-haired guardians of the secret crossroads
Euryale, Sthenno, Medusa
I stir, conjure, and call thee!
Come forth from the west and protect the bearer of this
    seal!
You who are covered in impenetrable scales, with serpent
    hair and hands of brass
Guard against all malicious spirits and sorceries
Be present and stand ready!
Oh, Hekate!
By your name I call forth the graces!
Beauteous ones who dance eternal through the heavens
Thalia, Euphrosyne, Aglaia
I stir, conjure, and call thee.
Come forth from the glades and attend your sorcerer!
Heal all harm that has been done by my enemies
And lead me on the paths of plenty
Hekate Propylaia
Hekate Phosphoros
Hekate Propolos
Protectress, Illuminator, and Guide
It is in your name I call the spirits
To ask for their favor, fury, protection, and grace.
It is by your power that it shall be done.
Hail to Hekate, Keyholder of the world.

The invocation follows a simple pattern: first it invokes Hekate
as the supreme goddess and then, in her name, calls forth the spirits.

These triple groups of spirits are invoked in this particular order as a type of defensive strategy. First the Fates are called upon to lend fortune's favor to the whole situation. Next the Furies are called upon to forcefully drive out the offending influence from our sphere. After the influence has been routed out by the Furies, we set up guard against further attack by invoking the Gorgons to stand guard. Finally we invoke the Graces to heal any damage done and ask for their benevolent blessing.

The symbol that is connected with this spell can be engraved onto metal, preferably silver, burned into wood, or made on parchment and carried. It can also be drawn over a door as a protection glyph or on the floor as a protective circle.

NEW EDITION COMMENTARY

In this chapter I provided a group of personal protections and cleansings, all of which are solid, and all of which I still use today.

The only thing that I want to add here is that if you are already under attack, protection is not enough. You need cleansing and purification to get rid of what is already affecting you. The baths all do this, and so does Hekate's wheel. I just don't think I stressed the point strongly enough.

My recommendation is to always start with a bath to purify yourself. A very simple formula that I didn't give here is a three-salt bath: equal parts Epsom salt, saltpeter, and table salt or sea salt. Pray to Hekate or whatever power you choose to rely upon for protection and empower the mixture, then wash yourself from the top of the head down to the feet. If you are old-school, you will do this in a basin, then throw the bathwater out to symbolize the removed condition leaving you, but if you're lazy like me, chances are you will just do this in the tub and let it go down the drain. That's fine, too.

After that you may want to work in some energetic cleansing. The simple "Conjuring the Column" I give to start both the Sphere of Hekas in the last chapter and the Invisibity ritual in this one can be done on its own as an excellent energetic cleansing and purification. You could easily add in some simple breathing exercises where you breathe in clean pure air and breathe out black smoky air. The Nine Purification Breath technique used in Tibetan yogas is just one example of this simple but effective procedure.

Whether you lay your protections before you cleanse or cleanse then purify doesn't matter all that much, but if you are under attack you want to make sure to do both. Cleansing with no protection will just allow whatever forces are assaulting you to return in force. Protection with no cleansing will block more influence from affecting you but might leave the spiritual infestation or infection already afflicting you to run rampant.

Chapter 4

PROTECTION FOR
THE HOME

Now that we have dealt with methods of personal protection, we will move on to protecting the home. Just as Superman needs his fortress of solitude when things get rough, a witch's home should be a refuge even amidst the strongest attacks. The home (and car and office) is in many ways a magickal extension of ourselves. If an attacker lacks a good personal item, such as hair or clothing, to use as a magickal link, the cunning sorcerer will usually target the home instead and use it as a giant magickal link. Throwing Goofer Dust or planting a gris-gris on someone directly is a bit more noticeable than going to his or her home in the dead of night and planting it on the door-step or burying something in the yard, and so it is one of the time-honored ways of delivering a curse.

Apart from attacks by other sorcerers, the home of a witch is often the site of many rituals that will attract all kinds of varied spirits and forces. Contrary to popular occult teachings, spirits and forces are not instantly and permanently shut off when the circle is closed or a banishing ritual is done. Nor should they be. A witch's home *should* be a house of the spirits, where not only can they be conjured and questioned, but they can also approach you in return. This is how a relationship with the intelligences and spirits is built, and we should not mistake the instructions for protecting the home as instructions for shutting off all contact with the other worlds, powers, and denizens. We should, however, have some defenses set up to repel forces that are hostile or draining to us, that may get snared into our home by our magickal actions. Most of us have many different visitors come and go from our home, not all of whom have been vetted and shown to be safe. We feel safe in receiving visitors because we have some kind of security at our disposal (even if it's only knowing how to dial 911) if one of our visitors gets threatening or violent. We must learn to do the same with the spirits.

I will be referencing the "home" in this chapter, but most of the instructions can also be applied to the car, to the office, or to anywhere else that you spend a lot of time. Likewise, instructions for the "house" are usually applicable to an apartment and what isn't able to be done to the letter can be altered with some ingenuity. Instructions that call for something to be buried in the yard, for instance, can also be buried in a potted plant in an apartment.

FLOOR WASH

The floor wash works for your home in the same way that your bath does for your body. Washes are a very old and traditional part of magick that are especially prevalent in hoodoo practice. There are floor washes to serve every magickal end—from stopping gossip, to drawing trade to brothels, to making peace—but we are concerned here only with those washes that are used in magickal defense.

A floor wash to repel harm is applied from the rear of the house toward the front door and out, as if you were gathering up the unwanted influence and pushing it out through the door. A floor wash for attracting is done exactly the opposite and moves from the front door toward the rear of the house. If your house or building has many floors, start from above and work down to repel, and the opposite to attract. If your house is carpeted, you can mix up a batch of the wash in a spray bottle and use it to spray the carpet, or if you are more traditional, you can use a feather or an aspergillum to sprinkle the wash onto the carpet. The general pattern of either back to front or front to back should be followed whichever method you use, and it will be necessary to map out your path through the house before you begin.

As with the bath, the floor wash is ideally made with water gathered from a natural source such as a river, spring, or collected rainwater. Water from the tap will do in a pinch, but water from a natural source is traditional and should be used if you can get it. A relatively small amount (a tablespoon to a cup) of ingredients is added to a gallon or more of water and prayed over fervently. If you don't want to add the ingredients directly because of the mess, you can often brew them into a tea and add that to the water.

I have listed some formulas that are useful in defensive and protection magick. Again, I have kept the formulas to simple three-ingredient washes. Those interested in more complex formulas are invited to consult the many magickal herbals:

To Clear Away Malefica
Pine needles
Saltpeter
Your own urine (first of the morning)

Exorcism Wash
Garlic

Pepper

Vinegar

Peace Wash
Sugar

Lavender

Rose water

Repelling and Keep-Away Wash
Witch's salt[1]

Valerian root

Broom

Spiritual Cleansing Wash
Powdered eggshells

Oak bark

Lemongrass

You can use these or other formulas whenever you think they are needed for a room or a whole house. It is a good practice to choose one good cleaning formula and use it with every new moon whether you are under attack or not, especially in your temple space. When you are done with your washing, you should take the excess wash and dirty water and dump it out the front door toward the east. As with baths, the wash is best done in the morning before dawn, but can be used at any time as needed. For instance, if someone whom you consider an enemy leaves your home, you can apply the "keep away" wash right after they leave to compel them not to return.

INCENSE

There is no more prevalent and archetypal aspect to magickal ritual than the burning of incense. Nearly every culture on Earth recognizes the spiritual power that certain herbs, resins, and woods have when burnt. By imbuing the material substance with our aspirations and desires, then burning it, it moves from the material to the intangible, and finally over into the spiritual dimension where our prayers are heard.

You can burn incense in a stationary holder, but if you are using it in a ceremony of cleansing or banishing you should use a censer or something that you easily can carry around. The pattern of censing with incense is the same as washing: back to front and out the door to expel, front to back to attract.

Incense recipes abound, and you should feel free to experiment during calm times with different formulas. When you are in dire need of defense or when someone else is relying on you are not the times to try out something new, so be sure to pick out a few successful recipes before you need them. Some excellent incense formulas that I have used are:

For General Cleansing, Protection, and Exorcism
Frankincense
Myrrh
Dragon's blood

For Reversing Harm
Mullein
Sage
Rue

For Calming Spirits
Camphor
Mint
Pine

Floor washes can be said to represent the two feminine elements: Water (the water for the wash) and Earth (the herbs, minerals, and other ingredients in the wash). Incense represents the male elements: Air (the smoke) and Fire (the burning). The combination of incense and floor wash is a very comprehensive way to imbue an environment with your will. As with the bath, the process is empowered by speaking a prayer or spell while washing or censing. Psalms are often used for this purpose in the various traditions of Christian witchcraft. Quotes from the Chaldean Oracles[2] lend themselves nicely to the process, as do the various Wiccan formulas for exorcism by saltwater and incense. I like the following formulae for protection, cleansing, and exorcism:

> By Earth the body of the Gods, by Water their flowing
> blood!
> By Air the Breath of the Gods, by Fire their burning spirit!
> I drive away all evil, harm, and hate!
> Apo Pantos Kakodaimonos!
> Hekas Hekas Este Bebeloi!
> Sigy! Sigy! Sigy!

Though I have included this spell in the chapter on home protection, it can just as easily be used with a bath/incense combination and applied directly to a person.

PROTECTION & REVERSAL MAGICK

POWDERS AND DUSTS

Apart from floor washing and censing, it is also traditional to lay powders to influence a place for good or for ill. Dusts and powders can consist of just one material purely or can be a combination of herbs, minerals, and even animal materials that are ground down and either used alone or mixed with a neutral powder base such as talcum. When dressing a room with powders you can either circle the perimeter or lay small piles in each of the four corners and one in the center. In some cases you will want to lay powders at strategic points such as doorways and windows.

The use of powders for protection was highlighted in the 2005 movie *The Skeleton Key* where Kate Hudson's character used redbrick dust to keep her enemies out of her room. I wouldn't bet on the dust's ability to work like it did in the movie, literally making enemies act as if an invisible wall were barring them entry, but it is a traditional practice and people all over the southern United States use it to protect their homes.

Though graveyard dust is often thought of as a material used in cursing, it can also be used for protection and many other positive purposes. It all depends on whose grave the dirt is taken from. Back when it was normal for people to build their own houses and pass them down through the family, it was not uncommon for people to use graveyard dust from the grave of a family member to protect the house, especially if the dirt could be obtained from the grave of the person who built the house, as they would have a special interest in protecting the property that they worked so hard on. To collect graveyard dirt, you cannot simply take it from the grave without giving anything back in return. A traditional offering would be some whiskey or a dime, and if you knew the family member in life, you could offer him something that he enjoyed in life as well. Take the dirt and sprinkle some in the four corners of your house and talk to the spirit, asking him to protect your house for you and keep away all harm. If you don't have access to the grave of a relative that you can rely on, you can also use the grave of a soldier. In every case of using graveyard dust for whatever reason, it is a good idea to do a divination to see if the spirit is willing to work for you.[3]

Cascarilla is also a valuable defensive tool. This is a white chalk made from powdered eggshells and is usually sold in small paper cups. Eggs represent the very stuff of life itself, and cascarilla enjoys a reputation in Santeria as a powerful protector. It can be used to draw protective symbols on walls or on the ground, and also on the body. Whenever I know that I will be in a magickally hostile environment or handling an object that someone thinks is fixed or cursed I draw bands around my arms with three crosses around through the band. I also mark the inside of my shoes with cascarilla crosses.

Apart from these single-ingredient powders, there are also herbal "condition" powders that are useful in defensive magick, such as Fear Not to Walk over Evil, and Fiery Wall of Protection, that can be purchased from any good botanica or occult store. Some recipes that I find useful are:

Protection against Malicious Witchcraft[4]
Trefoil
Saint John's wort
Dill
Vervain

To Establish Peace in the Home
Southern John root
Lavender
Pennyroyal

General Protection Powder
Wormwood
Solomon's seal
Blue cohosh

Any of these formulas, or others that you invent or research, can be made by powdering the herbs and mixing them into a powder base, such as talcum powder. I have included powders under the heading of protection for the home, but they can also be used on the person just like regular talcum powder.

AMULETS FOR THE HOME

Just as there are charms carried or worn on the person, there are amulets designed to imbue a place with their protective qualities. I already spoke about the use of iron in the last chapter and the use of iron fences to keep spirits in or out. Another use of iron as an amulet for the home is the ubiquitous horseshoe. There are many legends concerning the horseshoe, some of which are conflicting. For instance, some believe that the shoe must be hung with the points up or else the luck will run out. Others believe that it must be hung point down so that the luck pours into you. I hang mine point down and invite you to rely on your own intuition and inclination.

The origin of the horseshoe's use as an amulet is lost in antiquity, but some believe it originated as a clandestine symbol of Lunar Goddess worship and is thus connected to the underground witch cults. There is also a legend that the horseshoe's power comes from Saint Dunstan, who was a blacksmith before eventually becoming the Archbishop of Canterbury. The story is that he was asked to shoe the Devil's horse and placed a shoe on the Devil's hoof instead.

He would consent to take it off only if the Devil promised to never bother a home that had a horseshoe hanging as an amulet.

There are also horseshoe amulets made of blue glass with eyes on them that are a version of the malocco amulets that we talked about in the last chapter. These amulets are not only worn, but also hung in the home or car.

Mirrors are another very popular way of repelling evil from the home. Their use is very prevalent in China, where bagua mirrors surrounded by the eight trigrams are placed over doors and out windows to repel evil. In Morocco it is not uncommon to find large mirrors in the shape of hamsa hands or eyes that will repel evil in the same way. To use mirrors in protecting the home, you can purchase small round mirrors from a craft store and put them up near doorways and windows to reverse negative energy sent to you. If you wanted to get more complex, you could set the mirror in a small wooden disk and surround the glass with protection symbols such as in Figure 4.1 on p. 89.

Use a spoken charm, such as the following, when placing the mirror at its post:

> Mirror shield, where you are set
> No spell may pass, nor ill beget
> All devils captured in thy face
> Are driven backwards from this place
> By the name of fearsome Hekate
> And by my will, so shall it be.

Certain woods are also said to protect against occult attacks. In parts of England there is a custom of growing hedges of hawthorn and blackthorn to keep away spirits. Hawthorn is also the traditional wood used to make stakes to impale vampires upon, and in Bosnia

Figure 4.1 Mirror Protection Sigils

it is placed upon the navel to keep corpses from returning to life. Yew trees are also rumored to keep the dead at bay and are planted in graveyards for that very reason. The hanging of thorny branches of almost any kind over a doorway to keep away witches is another custom that is spread all across Europe and also exists amongst Native Americans. In England, rowan crosses bound with red thread are another popular amulet against witchcraft. All of these protective woods can be bound to the rafters and beams of a house to strengthen the structure against magickal attack.

Another classification of house amulets is those that are believed to frighten away demonic spirits. The best known of these, of course, is the gargoyle or Chimera, which can be seen on many buildings and churches in almost any major city. Gargoyles are used architecturally as a way to direct rainwater, but because of their often-fearsome appearance they have come to be thought of as protectors of the building and its inhabitants. In Tibet and Nepal, a Garuda image of metal or wood is often seen above the door. The Garuda is a fearsome mythical bird that routs out troubles caused by evil Nagas,[5] and the Garuda is most often seen with a serpent in its mouth to symbolize this.

Figure 4.2 Garuda Door Element

Another amulet in this class is the Trapa bicornis, which is the seed of a Chinese plant sometimes called the water chestnut[6] and looks somewhat like a Devil with horns or a bat. I have seen people use the seed for protection in Nepal and America as well, where it is known as a devil nut or bat nut. Generally, it is hung above the door so that it can frighten away evil in the same way that the Garuda and gargoyle do. I will talk more about these amulets and their use as spirit houses in Chapter 6, which discusses guardian spirits.

PROTECTION & REVERSAL MAGICK

Figure 4.3 Devil Nut

DECOYS

Some amulets are not designed to keep evil away but rather to act as decoys that absorb the hit in your place. One of the most famous of these types of amulets is the witch bottle. Hundreds of witch bottles have been found by archaeologists between England and Germany, and it was not uncommon for a household in the 1600s or 1700s to have one buried somewhere on the property. A witch bottle can be made with a glass or ceramic bottle, to which nine needles, nine pins, and nine nails are added. Other sharp objects, such as fish-hooks and razors, can be added as you see fit, as can lethal herbs, such as nightshade and hemlock. Finally, you need to add your own urine to the bottle. The urine attracts the spirit and spell looking for you, and the sharp objects entangle and destroy it. Some people place hair and fingernail clippings into the bottle as well, but I recommend against it, as they can be removed and used as magickal links against you if the bottle is found. I suppose that the urine could be removed as well and used against you, but it's difficult to remove when it dries up, not to mention very undesirable to work with if it's not yet dried up. The bottle is then sealed and buried somewhere on your property, usually under the walkway or doorstep. It is an old belief that if a witch who means you harm walks over the bottle, he or she will experience great pain on the spot, and even possibly die.

Another variant on the magickal decoy is the simple egg. To use this spell you should take a hard-boiled hen's egg in your right hand and circle the perimeter of the home three times clockwise. As you do so you can use the following spell as an incantation:

Seed of Life, to you I pray
No evil in your presence stay
In this sphere, where you are cast
No chaos or curse or crossing last
All hags and haunts and hunting dead
Be drawn from me to thee instead
By Hekate's power this charge I give
To guard the home in which we live.

After the egg has circled the house, you can put it in a box and bury it under your doorstep or wall it up in the house. You can also place it on your altar, where it will serve not only as a decoy but also a warning, as the egg is said to break if it absorbs an attack.

TRAPS

The last type of home protection we will consider is the spirit trap. Almost all cultures have methods for trapping or tangling spirits and spells. In Nepal and Tibet it is not uncommon to come across thread crosses that are built for this purpose. Threads of five colors are wound, representing each of the five elements. The threads are then empowered with pujas and dedicated to specific Tantric guardian deities. A similar process is used to demarcate boundaries with a circle made of the same five threads.

A very popular spell involves burying nine viburnum twigs, also known as devil's shoestring or hobble bush, in your walkway. While doing so, you utter a protective psalm or spell or can whisper a short charm to each one, such as:

Twisted, Tangled,
Hobbled and Bound,
Commit all Evil
To the ground.

Triangles are generally a shape that is believed to trap spirits. There is some evidence to show that the three-sided shape of the modern tent stake has its origins in Sumerian stakes that were used to nail down spirits. This tradition survives in Tibet and India as the famous phurba, or thunder nail, which has made appearances in mainstream movies such as *The Shadow* (1994) and *The Golden Child* (1986). In the phurba rituals, an effigy called a linga is placed in the center of a triangle that is drawn, either on paper or on the ground. Sometimes a triangular iron box is used. The obstacle-causing spirits, or dregs-pa, are then summoned through a series of mantras and mudras[7] and trapped in the triangle where they are dispatched with the phurba.

We find a similar use of the triangle in the Goetia, where the spirits are summoned into a triangle that is marked with various holy names such as the Archangel Michael's. The triangle is placed outside of the protective circle and the evoked spirits are compelled to appear within it and can be released only when the magician is ready.[8]

On the cover of this book is a triangular spirit trap that appeared to me during the series of Hekatean workings that inspired many of the spells in this book. The seal may be burned into an appropriate

Figure 4.4 Triangular Spirit Trap

wood such as oak or drawn on paper with dragon's blood ink. However it is made, the symbol should be consecrated with the following ritual.

On the new moon, an offering of food to Hekate should be laid out at the nearest crossroads to your home. It is best if a three-way crossroads is used, but if you can't find one, then a four-way will do. Also, if you cannot wait for the new moon because of a serious attack, you should go ahead and do it when your need is greatest. This offering should consist of foods sacred to Hekate such as red mullet fish, bread, raw eggs, cheese, garlic, cake, and honey. You can also include herbs such as aconite and dandelion root. (Please note that aconite is considered a deadly poison and should be treated with the conscientiousness that such a substance requires.)

Invoke Hekate from the heart:
Hail, many-named mother of the Gods, whose children
    are fair
Hail, mighty Hekate, Mistress of the threshold
You who walk disheveled and wild through tombs and
    cremation grounds
Cloaked in saffron, crowned with oak leaves and coils
    of serpents
You who are followed by hordes of ghosts, dogs, and
    restless spirits
I come to you for aid.
I call to thee by thy secret names:
Aktiophis, Ereshkigal, Nebotosoualeth
Empower this seal, and make it mighty
That it may ensorcel those spirits who cause harm
    and trouble
May the Empusae be trapped within it
May the Lamia be trapped within it
May the Mormo be trapped within it
May the Vrykolakas be trapped within it
May the Apotropaioi be trapped within it
May all manner of Specter, Phantoms, and Kakodaemon[9]
Be drawn into the triangles
Forever to live within the confines of the seal.
Hekate, Mistress of the Threshold,
Accept my offering and bless this seal.

The seal can then be placed in any and all points of entrance to the home, in doorways or windows, or under floorboards. Let intuition be your guide.

If you find that you need to draw a specific spirit into the seal, you can consecrate a fairly large version and take a mullein stalk that has been dipped in oil and place it in the center of the seal, where the two inner triangles touch. Light the stalk and, using words of your own choosing that fit the situation, summon the spirit into the seal. Bind it in the names of Aktiophis, Ereshkigal, and Nebotosoualeth.

With these methods at your disposal you should have no trouble making your home resistant to magickal attacks of almost any kind. Of course, the regular performance of the banishings, meditations, and offerings are actually your main defense. These practices done regularly in the home will impregnate the atmosphere with power, gain you spirit allies, and generally make the home itself a trigger to the mind that you are safe to focus and relax.

NEW EDITION COMMENTARY

Again, I think that everything here holds up. If I have to add anything, I would simply restate what I said about the last chapter: make sure to cleanse/purify your space and protect it. One without the other is shortsighted.

The progression in the book from chapter to chapter through escalating methods is intentional. We start with your baseline knowledge, then progress to regular practices that you should be doing to strengthen yourself overall. Then we move to personal protection and treatment in Chapter 3, and on to environmental protection and treatment in this chapter. There is an order to it that should be mirrored in practice.

Whether you are setting up protection against what you fear might happen, or whether you are addressing an ongoing situation, you want to cleanse and protect your person, then cleanse and protect your home environment. Even if you go about with amulets and shielding all the time, everyone needs a sanctum where they can take all that off and rest. That is what this chapter aims at providing.

Chapter 5

EXORCISM

The need for an exorcism arises when protection has either failed or has not been employed at all, and hostile intelligences have gained the upper hand and are adversely affecting a person or place. Simpler banishing rituals and blessings have not succeeded in expelling the presence and so something more must be done. An exorcist expels the presence by virtue of his or her spiritual authority. Indeed, the word exorcism comes from the Greek word *exorkizein* and means "to bind or adjure by oath." The oaths referred to are the oaths the exorcist has taken in the presence of the gods and by which power he can command the spirits.

Generally speaking, exorcism is the solution to one of two problems: *possession* or *obsession*.

Possession is the infestation of a person by an invading spirit. Symptoms range from the victim simply feeling the separate presence inside him, to a full displacement of the host personality where the spirit manifests through the body and voice of the affected. True possession is rare and difficult to deal with. The line between psychological and occult problems is very blurry in this area, and often a combination of both treatments is needed for a full recovery.

Obsession is far more common and can be defined as a persistent and intrusive hostile presence that makes itself known through various suggestive means. Obsession can affect a person or a place, and the symptoms can range from the simple feeling of an evil presence, to visions and paranoia, to physical phenomena, such as people being pushed down stairs or objects moving on their own. By far the most common complaint in cases of obsession is a weight on the chest while in bed at night, sometimes followed by temporary paralysis.

To be clear, cases of obsession are not just hauntings. It is not merely the presence of a neutral spirit or force that is cause for an exorcism, but a spirit or force that is hostile to humans and is working actively to our detriment. Strange and disturbing as a haunting may be to some, they are not attacks and are best handled with offerings, banishings, benedictions, and such.

Exorcism of any kind should not be undertaken lightly. Cases of personal possession in particular are best left to experts. Under no circumstances should an exorcism of a possessed person be attempted without exhausting the psychological and medical treatments first. If an exorcism is to be done, it should be coordinated with people in these fields. The fact that most Christian churches require the written approval of a bishop and a heap of evidence before an exorcism is undertaken should speak to the serious nature of the operation. Churches and individuals that offer exorcism without proper preparation often cause serious damage to their subjects, and one doesn't have to look far to find news reports of abuse and even deaths that occur during exorcisms. Because people undergoing exorcism sometimes react violently, the session should be taped and witnessed by several people. Everyone should know what to do in case of an emergency. Sedation or restraints may be necessary, which of course bring legal issues. People performing exorcisms have been accused of assault, and even murder. The 2005 movie *The Exorcism of Emily Rose* was loosely based upon the case of Anneliese Michel in Germany and points out some of the dangers inherent in the practice.

I cannot stress these points enough, and it is my hope that anyone reading this book who is approached by someone requesting an exorcism and claiming to be possessed takes these warnings into account. In fact, if these points were made to you for the first time while reading this, then you should not attempt an exorcism of a person at all without guidance from a more experienced person in the field.

Cases of obsession affecting either person or place are much more common than possession, and it is more likely that you will be confronted with having to perform an exorcism of this type than a genuine possession. While they do not share all the considerations that need to be taken into account that possession cases do, situations of obsession can still be dangerous and should not be taken lightly.

Exorcism is accomplished by a battle of wills, and, in order to win, your will must be linked with something beyond your own personal wants and desires. Your will must be identical to the will of the gods. The will of the gods or the Universe is manifesting through you, and you must have complete faith in that in order for the exorcism to be successful. When you speak, your words carry the weight of that will, and through that faith you can command an entity to vacate. It is not enough to *believe* that you can channel this will, you have to *know* it.

You should not attempt exorcism by yourself. Once, when attempting an exorcism of a house, I began to run a high fever and passed out. An assistant practically carried me out of the house, where we regrouped and went back in. We were eventually successful, but had I been alone, I don't know what would have happened. There should be a contingency plan for every possible situation. Once begun, an exorcism must be carried out until it succeeds, even if this means repeating the ceremony several times over the course of time. If exorcism is begun and then abandoned completely, the situation can get much worse than it was when you started.

After a lot of thought, I have opted not to include a specific ritual for exorcism in this book. Instead, I will give a general outline of what should be done. I have chosen to do it this way because I want to make it very clear that it is not the ritual that will do the job, but the person doing it. The most complex and time-honored rites carried out with theatrical precision will not work at all if the people performing it do not possess knowledge of their true will and access to the higher powers. Someone who does possess a combat-ready faith in himself as an agent of the higher powers can perform a very effective exorcism by doing little other than repeatedly telling the daemon to go and never return. Anyone ready to perform an exorcism will be able to find or construct a ritual using the following framework as a guide. If you can't put one together, then you aren't ready to perform one.

After your team has been assembled, you should gather in the place to be exorcised or around the person to be exorcised, and firmly state what is to be done: that you have gathered to drive out a hostile presence and will do so in the name of the higher powers. Each person should be asked by the leader if he or she is prepared, and if each person answers in the affirmative, you can proceed. This step must not be skipped. Even if everyone has agreed ahead of time that they are going to proceed, some people lose their nerve only when they are about to plunge in. It is here, in the presence of hostility, that each participant must dedicate him- or herself to the task at hand. If someone does bail out at this moment, no attempt should be made to convince him or her otherwise. If, after someone answers in the negative, you do not have sufficient people to proceed, you should abandon the rite and begin again when you have more people.

Exactly what higher powers you operate under is up to you. It is best if you have a long and established relationship with whatever deities or forces on which you will be relying. Many people suggest that it should be done in the religion you were born into. While I wouldn't go that far, I will say that formal initiation or consecration into a religion helps. Such initiations are actually tangible shields at the spiritual level and can serve you well in case difficulty and danger arise during an exorcism. If you do not possess such initiations, then at the very least you should have a rock-solid relationship with the powers that you are invoking.

Though it seems to be very much in vogue to do so these days, under no circumstances should you simply consult a dictionary of gods and goddesses and choose as many as you can find that fit the bill from different pantheons for your exorcism. It's *quality* not *quantity* that does the work here, and calling upon Mars, Marduk, Michael, Oggun, Horus, and Thor all at once will not serve you as well as calling upon just one deity or at least one pantheon with which you have a strong relationship.

Whatever power you are relying upon, be it a deity, saint, or Buddha, all present should pray fervently to that power that it may make itself known. Israel Regardie's advice to "enflame thyself with prayer" is what you should be striving for. Once the presence has been invoked generally, you should petition the power for strength and blessing. You should all feel that you have been made worthy champions by the power that you represent. You must have complete faith in this.

It is sometimes helpful to call upon especially martial spirits or forms of the power with which you are working. As an example, in the Judeo-Christian context after invoking God, it would be appropriate to invoke the angel Michael or Saint George. In a Buddhist context, after invoking the gurus and Buddhas, a wrathful Yidam such as Vajrakilaya or Hayagriva would be called upon. A strega who is calling upon Diana might then invoke the presence of Aradia or even a more wrathful goddess that Diana is connected with, such as Artemis.

A general address to all evil and ill can now be made. Do not focus on the specific malefic force yet, but rather command all evil and ill to abandon the person or place that is being exorcised. Do this repeatedly and in the name of the power that you have invoked. An exorcism is not the time to worry about being politically correct, so don't shy away from using words such as evil, unclean, and demon. Such words help in working your own power up to a fever pitch and clearly define that the time for bargaining and making peace is over; the goal of the exorcism is destruction or removal of the hostile entity, nothing else.

Now it is time to address the troublesome entity by name. Begin simply enough by asking what name you can call it. Demand to know. Command it to tell you. In cases of possession, it is possible (though not a guarantee) that the entity will speak through the possessed and you can converse with the intruder as you would the person in front of you. In cases of obsession, the obsessed person may hear the name spoken. It is also possible that you or a sensitive in your group will hear the name spoken either in the air or in your head. *You should not try to divine the name of the entity using a talking board or similar device.* Such tools give spirits a stronger foothold in the material plane and are meant only for friendly communication, which you are well beyond if you are performing an exorcism.

Do not linger too long on trying to get the entity's name; keep the ceremony moving on the offense. If you cannot perceive the entity's name, you should name it. This can be done on the spot or beforehand. The actual name matters little, and you should rely on your own inspiration when looking for a name. The idea of assigning a name brings the entity into the human sphere, making it easier to confront. You can say something along the lines of:

"Because you will not name yourself in a manner that we
can understand, I shall name you myself. By the power
of _____ I name thee _____. Thou art _____."

Once the offender is named, you should address it directly by that name. Adjure it in the name of your gods. Command it to leave. Be steady in the knowledge that you have the authority to do so. Doubts may occur in your mind. This is the entity battling you in your own psyche. Know that the laws of light and life are on your side. This is the only way to win.

Sometimes you will feel a sudden lightness in the air, and there will be general agreement that the entity has been exorcised. Sometimes, especially with weaker presences, it is hard to tell. A good way to bring the climax to a close is to write the name of the entity on a piece of paper and place it in a triangle. The triangle can be plain or a seal such as the one used in the Goetia or the Hekatean spirit trap that I presented in the last chapter. Whatever you use, the triangle should not be paper, as it will have to withstand the burning of the paper with the name on it.

Adjure the daemon in the name of Fire, and light the name paper. Adjure the daemon in the name of Water, and lustrate whatever is left. Adjure the daemon in the name of Earth, and throw salt at the ashes. Adjure the daemon in the name of Air, and blow the remains away with your breath. Trace an equal-armed cross in the air and adjure the daemon in the name of the gods and powers invoked during the ritual. Declare the spirit exorcised, expelled, and banished to such an extent that not even its name exists. Sweep up the ashes of the name paper and take them out of the building immediately. Eventually, you can dump them in a river, scatter them to the wind, or bury them at a crossroads.

Whether you end with the burning of a name paper or not, at the end of the rite you should thank the powers that were invoked and take a few moments to praise them.

Banish the room immediately, and place protective wards and amulets such as the ones discussed in the previous chapters both in the building that was used for the exorcism and on the victims. It is a good idea for all to take protective and purifying baths for a few days after the exorcism and to use a floor wash on the rooms involved.

Traditionally, incense is used during the exorcism, and you should feel free to use one of the recipes from Chapter 4 or any sharp-smelling incense that you like. Avoid herbs such as dittany of Crete and mullein, which are used as materializing incenses.

The person or place that was the target of the exorcism should be monitored for several weeks, and they should be instructed to record any strange occurrences or relapse of symptoms. It is not uncommon for an exorcism to have to be performed more than once, so you may need to repeat the process three or more times. I strongly recommend videotaping or at least making an audiotape of the ritual, and I would like to again reiterate my advice that cases where a person is possessed are to be treated with the utmost care. They should be handled by an expert and in cooperation with medical and mental-health professionals.

NEW EDITION COMMENTARY

Exorcism comes from the Greek word *orkizo*, which mean to bind by oath. You may notice that we use this word *orkizo* to summon the guardians in the Sphere of Hekas ritual in chapter 2. People tend to think that evocation, the summoning of spirits to appear before you, and exorcism, the forced expelling of spirits from a person or place, are opposites, but they aren't. They are done through the same process: binding the spirit by oath.

To do this you need to possess the spiritual authority to command a spirit. This can be authority vested in you through initiation or consecration, it can be accomplished through making strong allies or resonance with a power that you can call upon, or rarely it can be earned through your own spiritual work and transformation. You are, after all, a spirit.

Some attempt to invoke this authority ritually just before an operation, and this can work, but it's not ideal. If you are entering into a confrontation with a spirit, you should have something more solid behind you than a single ritual invocation declaring yourself to be Moses or visualizing yourself in a God-Form for the first time.

Some readers were confused at my decision not to include an exorcism script with this chapter. After all, at the end of this book I teach bindings, confusion spells, and expelling rites that some would classify as curses, so why am I shy about encouraging exorcisms?

I am not worried about you hurting yourself, or someone that you are in a confrontation with. I am worried about people picking up this book, or books like it, and attempting to exorcise patients and clients and making things worse. A lot of people have been killed or seriously injured during "exorcisms" carried out by the ill-prepared or ill-intentioned upon clients that are at their most vulnerable point. I don't mean to be overly negative, but the readers and students that have lobbied me the hardest to provide exorcisms are often those I would least trust to perform one. Too many people are far too eager to hang out a sign and play out their fantasies of fighting evil with magick.

Still, it is perhaps a failure of the book to not provide an example to work from, so now there is a Hekatean exorcism in the appendixes that you can use as it is written or as a base for longer exorcisms of your own.

Realize this: exorcism is a confrontation. There is always push-back. If all you have known of magick is casting spells that either work or don't work, or prayers that you assume reach a God or Goddess that is more than capable of handling anything and everything, you might find yourself shocked at just how much a spirit is able to push back. You can go in with all your rituals thinking you have a solid plan of how it's going to turn out, but that usually gets thrown out the window as soon as things get real. Since getting rid of a spirit through exorcism is a fight, perhaps it's best to close these notes with a quote from Mike Tyson: *"Everyone has a plan until they get punched in the mouth."*

Chapter 6

SPIRIT GUARDIANS
AND SERVITORS

Throughout the book we have been talking about spirits, both in terms of being sources of potential attack and also their employment in strategies of defense. Before moving forward, I wanted to take a moment and talk about the nature of spirits and magick in general. Because so much of what magicians and witches deal with is invisible to the untrained eye, it is tempting for many people to try to find psychological explanations for traditional aspects of magick. In this view, spells aren't aimed at actually making changes in the outside world, but rather for "self-empowerment." Spirits are not viewed as discarnate intelligences, but as aspects or projections of the mind.

In his article "Is Wicca Under a Spell?"[1] Carl McColman quotes Australian sociologist Douglas Ezzy regarding the effect of spells themselves:

Spell books "encourage individuals to take control of their lives through self-exploration and self-affirmation."

Furthermore, "performing magical spells functions as a way of re-discovering the enchanted and mysterious aspects of life."

McColman further interprets this:

In other words, spells are more than just magical recipes for getting your own way; they are miniature rituals designed to foster a sense of mystery and wonder (what Ezzy calls "enchantment") in everyday life, and to evoke a positive sense of power and hope in the spell-caster's life. Even if casting a spell doesn't make you rich or win you love, it could give you hope that such blessings really are possible in your life.

Thus, a spell to help you get a job will perhaps build your confidence but not affect the mind of the interviewer or the hiring process directly. The claim is that the magick is providing mystery, wonder, and self-affirmation, and the hope that you can achieve the spell's end. This is all very wonderful, and indeed magick can provide all these things, but it is clear that magicians and witches throughout history expected more from their spells than a cathartic ritual, and I stand with them![2]

Spirits, too, are seen by many respected magicians in the modern day as little more than psychological projections. Even the spirits in the ancient grimoires such as the Goetia, the oldest of the books in the Lemegeton,[3] are given this treatment by modern writers. Lon Milo DuQuette in his essay "Demons Are Our Friends" states: "Like it or not, we all come hardwired with a complete set (twelve six-packs) of Goetic Demons."

In this attitude, he is following the lead of no less authority than Aleister Crowley himself, who wrote in his introduction to his translation of the Book of the Goetia of Solomon the King: "The spirits of the Goetia are portions of the human brain."

While I respect the writings of both of these magicians greatly, I must disagree. My experience is that while certain spirits seem to be able to interface with our brains and speak to us through them, they are not limited by this and can act in ways that are far outside the realm of being portions of the human brain. But just as the perception of the ordinary person is limited by his or her lack of belief in spirits and magick, so the perception of many magicians and witches is limited by their psychologically oriented views.

These views sometimes carry over into the conjuration itself. Once, when planning a Goetic evocation of the spirit Vassago at Thelesis Camp in Philadelphia,[4] where I would have been the evoking magician and a sister of the group would have been the scryer, someone in the group became very concerned over "whose Vassago" we would be summoning into the triangle—mine or the scryer's. When I explained that we were looking at this traditionally and that Vassago was Vassago and not just a part of someone's psyche thrown into a scrying mirror, he looked deeply concerned about my sanity. This type of thinking will place severe limitations on the ceremony itself and likely reduce it to the purely psychological event that people are expecting.

Whatever your view on the spirits, it is clear that old grimoires were written for their rituals to be performed as if the spirit were a separate, discarnate intelligence, and not just a part of your brain. Even if you think that the spirit is a part of your psyche, and the ceremony works via your own belief, it follows that if you treat the spirit as a separate entity that you are summoning, you will be able to get more worked up over the process than if you go into it as some psychological trick, and thus achieve greater success no matter what the spirit's true nature.

In my practice, experience has led me to embrace the more traditional view of spirits: that where there is space, there is awareness, and this awareness manifests as varying classes of beings possessing different natures and powers. Some are localized, some are not; some can speak to you only using information in your mind to express themselves, some can speak to you as clearly as if they were a person standing in front of you. Some have influence over the material world, some do not. Whatever your personal views and beliefs on the subject, I encourage you to treat them in ritual according to this traditional view, as that is what experience has taught me yields the best results. Besides, as one of my magickal mentors Cliff Pollick once told me: "There is nothing like getting bitten on the ass by something that you didn't quite believe in." If and when that happens, you may find you need this book more than you thought.

GUARDIAN SPIRITS

Just as spirits can sometimes cause harm, so can they defend against it. The practice of invoking gods and spirits for aid is common in almost all religions, and one doesn't need training in witchcraft to pray for help. While general prayer can sometimes be effective, remarkably so in some cases, the sorcerer will want to employ some surer methods of defense than just leaving the situation in the hands of the gods. Thus we seek to develop a relationship with various guardian spirits, and to learn the methods whereby they are summoned and convinced to aid us.

In most magickal worldviews there are very powerful, or even omnipotent, deities that are an object of veneration or worship.

These beings are typically seen as being somewhat removed from the physical world and thus not very in touch with the goings-on of everyday life. Because of this distance between the gods and man, there are often sets of spirits that are petitioned for aid with material problems and are thought to be more likely to intercede in our affairs than the high gods. We have already touched upon the defensive use of the spirits of departed humans through the agency of their graveyard dust in a previous chapter, but there are other types of spirits that can be employed by the cunning magician.

In Tibet, for instance, there are beings known as dharmapalas, most of whom were spirits in Tibet that received blood sacrifices before Buddhism was brought to the Land of Snows in the 8th century. Because they knew that Buddhists were against animal sacrifice, they caused many problems for the King of Tibet, who was trying to build a monastery and establish Buddhism. The magician Padmasambhava was called upon to travel through Tibet and tame these spirits. Because these spirits were very connected to the material plane, he pressed many of them into service as guardian spirits and promised that they would be offered tormas (cakes) that would replace the blood sacrifices to which they were accustomed. To this day, Tibetan Buddhists offer cakes that are shaped and colored like bloody heads and such to appease these dharmapalas.[5]

In Catholicism and Catholic-influenced magick such as hoodoo, we have angels and saints interceding, which are seen as more effective than calling upon God himself, because, like the dharmapalas, they are more connected to the material plane and to the human experience. In vodou, the loa serve the same function, most of whom were human ancestors that have been elevated to a higher level and now serve the community. It is well known that European witches have called upon all sorts of familiar spirits for aid and have a long history of dealing with spirits such as the fey and sidhe. The medieval grimoires of ceremonial magick, which were written primarily for use by Christian clergy, are filled with catalogues of spirits that were known to be fast and powerful in fulfilling the requests of the magicians who evoked them.

Because these spirits are not as removed from the human condition as the high deities, they are also not as enlightened and thus can sometimes be dangerous to work with, and so they must be treated with a firm hand. In the case of Tibet, although the dharmapalas are oath-bound, there are retinues of spirits that serve each one, some of whom are considered dregpa, which means that they are arrogant and easily offended. Because of this, whenever the dharmapalas are evoked in ritual, the person doing it takes the god-form of a powerful enlightened Buddhist god called a yidam. Usually this yidam is itself very fearsome in appearance and is therefore threatening to the lower spirits.

In the grimoires, we see similar tactics used for binding the demons that can sometimes get unruly. In this case the various names of God are invoked and the demon, which is often secretly a Pagan deity in disguise, is forced into appearing in a comely form and behaving politely. Often these conjurations and bindings are issued in an increasingly more dire and threatening order. The Goetia even goes so far as to suggest placing the spirit's sigil inside a box and burning it if the spirit refuses to appear.

Whatever tradition you come from, the spirits are generally called upon via some symbol or sound that is connected with them. In the East, a mantra is most often assigned to a guardian, and someone wanting to invoke the protection of a particular spirit might meditate on the spirit's mantra repeatedly. It would not be uncommon to recite a mantra 10,000 or more times in order to request the aid of a dharmapala.

In the West, spirits are more often connected with sigils than with mantras, though the name of the spirit is also a powerful link. The word *sigil* comes from the Latin *sigillum* and can be translated as a "seal" or "signature." The seal of a spirit is not only its signature, though, but also its phone number and address rolled into one. In some cases, the seal of a spirit is synonymous with the spirit itself, and thus the presence of a spirit exists wherever its seal is present.

The methods of obtaining sigils for spirits vary widely. In some cases, the seal is a combination of letters (often the spirit's name) bound together so that the individual letters are all present but not immediately apparent. In some cases a spirit's name can be traced on a tablet, such as the Golden Dawn's Rose Cross Lamen and the Agrippa's planetary kameas. In the case of the latter, the numbers of the magickal squares that make the kameas are assigned letters according to Hebrew, and the sigil is traced using a circle to mark its beginning and a line to mark its end.

Some sigils are more pictographic, such as the veves of Haitian vodou. For example, Papa Legba's veve contains a crossroads and a cane, Erzulie's is a heart, and Gran Bwa's veve looks like a tree person. Each of these veves conveys something of that particular lwa's nature and iconography, executed in an artistic style heavily influenced by French ironwork. Some of the seals in the greater Key of Solomon and the Black Pullet are also very picture oriented and may even have very blatant pictures of rings and people contained within them.

There are also cases where a sigil is revealed directly by a spirit or god. When received clearly, without too much intrusion from the receiver's conscious mind, these are the most powerful sigils, especially if you were the one to whom the sigil was revealed. Automatic writing, scrying, and oneiric sorcery are the most common modes by which these sigils are obtained from the spirits and can be employed by you to whatever extent your talent allows.

There are a number of different ways with which the sigil of a spirit can be worked. Sometimes they are worn as talismans or placed in the home, and the name of the spirit and any associated prayers or conjurations that are traditional are spoken while contemplating the seal. Other methods involve making offerings to the sigil, such as would be the case with the aforementioned veves.

As I write this, I have a candle in front of me that has the veve of Papa Legba painted on it in red. Before I began writing today, I laid a glass of bay rum in front of the candle and called Papa by one of his songs and then asked him to clear the obstacles that often arise during the day that interrupt my writing. In exchange for his service, I will offer him a coconut and more rum later, as well as this mention in the book in order to increase his renown.

If you choose to call upon a traditional spirit from an established magickal system, you should make every endeavor to reasonably follow the protocols of that system. This is particularly important in approaching spirits from traditions that still have a very active and traditional cult that has not had to be reconstructed, such as vodou, Santeria, Buddhism, and shamanism. Do *not* assume that the spirits will be cooperative and understanding if you approach them in the wrong way. If the spirit requires offerings, make sure those offerings are consistent with its nature. If the tradition requires that you be initiated to a certain level before approaching that spirit, I strongly recommend that you undergo that initiation before asking it for aid. At the very least, you should consult someone who has a background in that tradition or has dealt with that spirit before. Eclecticism is all well and good, but it must be done with intelligence and respect.

As an example of how this kind of thing can go horribly wrong, a witch in New York whom I am acquainted with decided to invoke the aid of the orishas after reading only a book or two on Santeria. He didn't know much of Santerian ritual structure, so he used a format similar to that of ceremonial magick and evoked orishas into the four quarters according to their elemental attributions. In the West he invoked Yemaya, as she is a goddess of the ocean, and West is associated with the element Water. In the North he invoked Oya, who is associated with mountains and thunder and also the grave, which seemed a perfect fit for the quarter associated with the element Earth. The problem is that in the Yoruban traditions these two goddesses hate each other because Yemaya tricked Oya into trading dominion over the ocean for dominion over the grave. Most botanicas won't even put their candles on the same shelf! This unwise individual began to see signs of the heavy crossed conditions that he brought on himself almost immediately. He eventually lost his job and suffered many health problems until he finally got a trained santero to intervene for him.

This kind of problem doesn't exist only in African-derived magick. I am aware of a similar problem that was caused by an American who was initiated into the practice of two dharmapalas that conflicted: Dorje Shugden and Ekajati. Ekajati is a Nyingma[6] dharmapala, and Shugden is from a small sect within the Gelugpa school. This spirit Dorje Shugden is so sectarian that the Dalai Lama has asked everyone in the Gelugpa school to stop propitiating him. Unfortunately, he is known for being very quick-acting in material matters and so some sects still give his initiation. The American in question had to undergo a long process to be free from the influence of Shugden, a spirit that she had no idea was hostile to the other schools.

If you choose not to work with a spirit from an established tradition, there are many ways to contact spirits yourself, from which you can then get names and sigils. If you are diligent with your offering rituals, such as those provided in Chapter 2, you may notice certain presences hanging around, and you can reach out to these beings and ask if they are willing to work as protective spirits for you. How exactly you do this depends largely upon your own talents and the capacity of the spirit involved. Some people will be able to establish direct contact psychically; some will need to rely upon divination for the answers. Sometimes a question asked during the day will be answered in a dream or when you are hovering between being asleep and awake and thus more sensitive to the influences of the invisible. Trance states can also be induced by over-breathing, meditation, self-hypnosis, chemicals, or any combination thereof.

Certain people, ceremonial magicians especially, would recommend strongly against contacting whatever spirits show up at your offerings or are just hovering about the landscape, writing it off as "ignorant spiritualism." Their argument is that the spirits in the grimoires have been evoked successfully for many years and their natures are already known, whereas whatever is lurking around the corner could be dangerous and is, at the very least, not to be trusted.

While I respect the fact that many people feel this way, I don't find the argument to hold much water. For one thing, many of the spirits in the grimoires that magicians like to use have natures that are anything but friendly and ready to serve. If you are going to go so far as to burn a sigil and ostensibly torture a spirit listed in a grimoire because it is so reluctant to appear, how much less cooperative could a local spirit be?

As for trust, while I agree that it's dangerous to trust local spirits blindly, I think it's dangerous to trust *anyone* blindly. There are many spirits in the grimoires that are devious by nature. The Goetia warns about the spirit Berith, for instance, as a spirit that is not to be trusted no matter what bindings you place on him. How much worse could you do on your own, talking to what appears at your offerings or in your local places of power?

The last hole in this argument is that these grimoires and spirits were contacted by somebody else first. Someone divined the name and seal, and then wrote the grimoire. That's not very different from working with various unknown spirits. Sticking to only those spirits that are in the grimoires or known traditions is somewhat like sticking with people listed in a "Who's Who" guide for all your friends. I wouldn't do that, would you?

Another way to contact a protective spirit is to pray and ask the gods to send one to you. Certain spirits and angels can also put you into contact with familiar spirits from the legions that they rule over. The aforementioned Goetia, for example, promises that many spirits such as Marax, Malphas, Sabnock, Shax, and Alloces all *give good familiars*" when asked. The spirits invoked in the banishing ritual from the second chapter—Abaek, Pyrhum, Ermiti, and Dimgali— all were revealed to me directly by asking Hekate to send protective spirits. There are seals and further rituals for each of them, but that will have to wait for a future book. In the meantime, they can be visualized and called upon either individually or as a group, according to the formula given in the banishing ritual.

In the chapter on home protection, I touched a bit on amulets that represent a fierce presence to scare away spirits such as the garuda door amulets of Nepal and Tibet, the devil or bat nut of American hoodoo, and the European gargoyle. Each of these items has the appearance of some kind of wrathful being that is dedicated to protecting the location in which they are set. As with so many amulets, their magickal potency is derived from their appearance, and it is believed that their form alone is enough to make them effective. They can be used as-is, or they can be awakened through energized prayer and spell work, but in general the item is not believed to be a spirit in and of itself. There are rites, however, wherein a spirit can be called to an object, which can be placed as a guardian in the home or even worn on the person.

The idea that spirits can inhabit physical objects is an old one and goes back to the earliest prehistoric shamanic practices. Binding a spirit to an object either temporarily or permanently has the benefit of giving the spirit a foothold in the material plane and also provides an easy way for you to contact the spirit to give it instructions and make offerings to it. Some people are uncomfortable with the idea of binding spirits to objects, thinking that it traps the spirit against its will, but this isn't necessarily the case. The nature of spirits is sometimes said to be like fire, and like a flame it can spread from one lamp to another without diminishing the flame from which it was taken. This explains why spirits, such as the four archangels, can be called upon effectively by multiple people at multiple times, and why objects such as idols and seals are treated as if they are *inseparable* from the spirit itself, even if multiple objects exist.

Of course, there are cases where the spirits are thought to be trapped in their entirety by very powerful sorcerers, such as when King Solomon supposedly bound up the seventy-two demons of the Goetia in a vessel of brass and when the Fifth Dalai Lama did the same to Dorje Shugden. In both of these cases, though, the spirits were later released by less proficient mages.

Objects such as the gargoyle, devil nut, and garuda all make excellent objects in which spirits can be placed. Paul Huson, in his excellent book *Mastering Witchcraft*, gives a ritual whereby a spirit, or *magistillus* (Latin for "little master"), is attracted into a mandrake root or an alraun and made to serve as a guardian of the hearth. The mandrake, or mandragore, gets its name because the root resembles a human form, whereas an alraun is a humanoid figure carved from rowan wood. More complex spirit houses can also be made, such as the Palero's nganga, which often takes the form of a cauldron with various objects, such as machetes and sacred woods, in it that assist the inhabiting spirit.

The following ritual is for the creation of a spirit house that will serve as home to the spirit Apoxias, who is another protective spirit that was revealed to me by Hekate. Apoxias appeared to me in the shape of a man with mirrored eyes and dark greenish-black skin. He carried a bell in one hand and a long razor-sharp sword in the other. He is charged by Hekate with standing guard over anyone who is unjustly attacked and is an excellent watchmen and guard.

His spirit house should be made from a bottle that is colored dark green.[7] The bottle should be exorcised with incense and saltwater before beginning. The bottle should be filled with dirt from the following places in the following order:

1. Dirt from a cemetery (not from a particular grave, just from the ground)

2. Dirt from a police station

3. Dirt from a bank

4. Dirt from a church (or temple or Masonic hall, you get the idea . . .)

5. Dirt from a government building

6. Dirt from the mountains or the highest ground around

7. Dirt from the shore of a lake or the beach

8. Dirt from a store

9. Dirt from a crossroads

The dirt from all these places should be from as close to your home as possible. You need only a little from each place, and the bottle should be only half full when you are finished. Next add the following items to the bottle:

1. Oak twigs

2. Pine needles

3. Blackthorn

4. Dandelion

5. Poppy seeds

6. Black mustard seeds

7. The hair of a black dog

8. Three razor blades

9. A small bell

The oak is for protection. The pine needles are for cleansing. The blackthorn is for tangling up obstructions. The aconite is poison and is also sacred to Hekate. The poppy seeds cause confusion, and the black mustard seeds cause harm to enemies. The hair of a black dog is also sacred to Hekate and grants Apoxias access to canine spirits that can track and hunt down offending presences. The razor blades symbolize the spirit's sword, and the bell represents the spirit's bell with which he simultaneously warns of attack and confuses his enemies.

On the outside of the bottle you should paste four mirrors to face the four directions. These simultaneously represent the eyes of the spirit and his ability to reverse harm back upon the sender. A small chain and padlock can be added to the outside to represent chains with which to bind your enemies.

Finally, you should prepare his seal on parchment but keep it outside the bottle for now.

Figure 6.1 Seal of Apoxias

If you can perform the rite on a new moon at a three-way crossroads, that is best. If not, then you can perform it in your home or someplace else that you find powerful. Wherever you decide to perform it, the ceremony must be performed on a new moon.

Begin by laying out a supper to Hekate such as was described for charging the spirit trap. It should include foods sacred to Hekate such as red mullet fish, bread, raw eggs, cheese, garlic, cake, and honey. You can also include herbs such as aconite and dandelion root as garnish. You should perform a banishing, such as the one from Chapter 2 or another formula of your choosing. After the banishing, sit for a moment in silence.

When you feel that you have entered into a receptive state, you should light some incense sacred to Hekate, such as a blend of myrrh, mugwort, and mullein. Call to Hekate using the following incantation while staring intently at the seal of Apoxias.

Hail, many-named mother of the gods, whose children are
    fair
Hail, mighty Hekate, mistress of the threshold
You who walk disheveled and wild through tombs and
    cremation grounds
Cloaked in saffron, crowned with oak leaves and coils of
    serpents
You who are followed by hordes of ghosts, dogs, and restless
    spirits
I come to you for aid.
I call to thee by thy secret names: Aktiophis, Ereshkigal,
    Nebotosoualeth
Mighty Hekate, send your angel Apoxias to inhabit this house
May he dwell within it and find all his weapons waiting
May he stand guard over my home, my family,
And all those I love and hold dear
May he stand firm against the powers and principalities of
    evil
May he turn back the tides of invading daemons
May he drive out those who conspire against me
May he hunt down the attackers where they dwell
And bring the battle to their door
Hail, many-named mother of the Gods, whose children are
    fair
Hail, mighty Hekate, mistress of the threshold
Send to me your spirit this night.

At this point you should focus intently on the seal of Apoxias.
Hold the seal over the incense smoke and chant the following charm
at least one hundred times (one hundred being a "hekad") to bring
him through his seal:

PROTECTION & REVERSAL MAGICK

IO APOX-IAS IO HO!
(ee-oh ah-pohks ee-as ee-oh ho!)

At some point you will feel the presence of the spirit enter the seal. This feeling differs according to our individual gifts and capacities, but can range from a simple feeling of not being alone, to the sensation of many invisible doors opening all at once, to something visible such as the lines of the sigil suddenly moving or seeming to appear in 3-D. Even if you receive the sign of his presence immediately, you should complete the one hundred recitations as an offering and way to affirm his presence. If you don't receive the sign, you should continue reciting until you do.

When you are done, you should place the sigil inside the bottle and close it up. Burn a black candle on top of the bottle, and in your own words thank Hekate and Apoxias for heeding your call. Place the bottle on your altar or on a shelf in your home. Every new moon you should burn some incense as an offering to the spirit and pray to him in your own words to continue protecting your home, family, and friends. You should also pay attention to omens and dreams, as well as anyone acting out of sorts around you. Apoxias is very good at making people with secret plans against you show their hands before they are ready to play them. He is also a very fierce protector, so those witches who believe in taking a very light-handed approach to defense, and would rather endure harm than risk harming an attacker themselves, should avoid this spirit entirely. Apoxias is not a pacifist.

As a last word, when dealing with spirits of any type, you should be aware that you are opening your life up to relationships with the other worlds. Like all relationships, it works two ways. The spirits will come when you call, but don't be surprised if they start calling you back on their own. Magick happens everywhere, not just within the confines of a circle. This relationship is a blessing and is the only way to learn the magick that can't be taught in books, but those not ready to handle this should avoid working with the spirits at all.

ARTIFICIAL SPIRITS

Apart from the use of spirits and intelligences that are attracted to the witch through conjuration or offering, there are also methods for creating artificial spirits. An artificial spirit is made from energy that is shaped and programmed by the witch, much like an artificial intelligence computer program. They are created for long- and short-term use and are known by many names. In traditional European witchcraft, an artificial is sometimes known as a *fetch* or *bud-will*. In ceremonial magick they are often called egregores, or when constructed from one or more of the four elements, artificial elementals.

One of the most famous examples of a magician creating a spirit for defense is the golem. In the year 1580, a Kabbalist named Rabbi Loeb is rumored to have created an artificial spirit that inhabited and animated a physical form called a golem. A Catholic priest named Taddeush was planning to accuse the Jews of Prague of ritual murder, which would start a backlash against the Jewish community that would result in many deaths. Rabbi Loeb heard about it and, to avert the danger, directed a dream question to heaven to help him save his people. He received his answer in a Hebrew code: *Ata Bra Golem Devuk Hakhomer VeTigzar Zedim Chevel Torfe Yisroel.* The literal meaning of this is: "Make a golem of clay and you will destroy the entire anti-Semitic community." Through the Gematric[8] interpretation of this phrase, the rabbi was able to decipher the actual formula for doing just that. The golem was given life by writing one of the names of God, *EMETH*, on its head. Stories vary about how the golem accomplished his task—some say it went berserk and had to be destroyed, some say that it only killed the priest and was then put to rest. The golem was deactivated by wiping off the E from the name on its forehead to change it from *EMETH* to *METH*, which means "dead" in Hebrew. The golem's body was sealed in a secret passage in a synagogue where it is said to remain to this day. Some believe this story was the inspiration for the Mary Shelley classic *Frankenstein*.

Another famous story involving the creation of an artificial spirit comes to us through Alexandra David Néel, the French explorer and author who penetrated Tibet in the 1920s and traveled the country disguised as a beggar and a lama. In her book *Magic and Mystery in Tibet*[9] she describes her creation of an artificial spirit called a tulpa, which roughly translates to "Mind Emanation" in Tibetan. In her story, she seals herself up in a cave and concentrates on creating a short, good-natured monk. After a few weeks, she feels that her monk is sufficiently manifest and she leaves the cave. The tulpa-monk follows her on her travels and is even seen by other members of her traveling party from time to time. The problems arise when the monk begins changing out of her control. His appearance shifts from being portly and good-natured to being gaunt and sinister. Realizing that her creation has gotten away from her, she decides to dismantle the monk, but accomplishes this only at great effort over the course of several months.[10]

There is even one case where an artificial spirit is treated as one of the chiefs of a whole magickal order! The Fraternitas Saturni in Germany at one time regarded an egregore named GOTOS (acronym for Gradus Ordinis Templi Orientis Saturni) as a secret chief. This egregore was fed into by everyone in the order and thus was somewhat of a group mind that could then be called upon to advise the order with the weight of its collected wisdom.

In the late 1980s, the use of artificial spirits became extremely popular amongst people interested in chaos magick, where the spirits are generally known as servitors. Whatever you want to call them, their construction and use are more or less the same. First, you must decide upon the function you wish them to perform; in our case, we are concerned with magickal defense and protection, but they can be made for almost any purpose. In general, artificial spirits are meant to be temporary and are designed to dissipate upon the completion of their task or upon a certain date. Permanent servitors can be constructed but must be carefully looked after and fed with energy to keep them in line, lest they begin to take their nourishment, and thus their programming, from elsewhere, as with the case of the runaway tulpa mentioned previously.

Before construction, decide upon a form. The form is limited only by imagination and should, in some way, indicate its function. A servitor made to warn of danger, for instance, could take the shape of a cloud of eyes and ears, and a servitor meant to guard a door could take the form of a knight in armor. Whatever you choose, you should be aware that the servitor may take on the characteristics of its form. If you want a servitor to charge into battle, don't make it cute and cuddly; similarly if you are afraid of causing harm in your response to danger, do not make it into the form of a bear.

You should then decide on a name and sigil that will represent the servitor. The name should represent its function in some way. If you do want a name that will indicate its function, you can choose one word and jumble the letters or pick a combination of words that you condense. The word *protector*, for instance, could be made into the name "Rectoport," and the words *binder of harm* can be made into the name "Binderham" by removing the word *of* and the repeating letter *r* from harm. An artificial spirit created primarily from an elemental or planetary force can be named with a word that recalls that force. Madim, for instance, is the Hebrew name for Mars and could be used as a name for a servitor made with energy emanating from that planetary sphere. Of course, if you feel inspired to name it something else, go right ahead. A friend of mine named his protective servitor Phil and claims great success with him.

A sigil can be constructed from one of the previously described methods, such as by combining letters into a symbol wherein the individual letters are not immediately apparent. You can also trace a sigil upon the kameas or Rose Cross Lamen if you know how. You can also make a chart of your own construction and trace a sigil on it. For example, you can make a 5 × 5 graph and fill it in with English letters according to your own inspiration, using *I* to also represent the letter *J* as it does in Latin.

The following methods could be used to make sigils for a servitor named Binderham.

Q	Y	N	L	B
C	P	E	T	V
H	I	A	O	D
K	Z	U	W	R
F	S	M	X	G

Figure 6.2 Letter Chart

Figure 6.3 Sigil Traced on Letter Chart

Figure 6.4 Combined Letter Sigil

Though it's not strictly necessary, I find it useful to write the name and sigil of the spirit on a piece of paper. This paper forms a magickal link and home for the spirit and can be used to feed the servitor and issue further instructions. The spirit's orders and other symbols appropriate to the working can be added to the paper as well, as can oils and powders consistent with the nature of the spirit. If you are planning to keep the spirit around long term, you can engrave the sigil and name onto a statue or other object that will then serve as a powerful guardian.

To actually construct the spirit you have to set a place a few feet in front of you where the spirit will manifest. I always place a triangle in this spot to help the manifestation of the spirit, and if you are using a paper or other object to serve as a connection to the spirit, then you can place it in the spot where the spirit will manifest. You should banish the space that you are working in or set up circle according to whatever methods you normally use.

Begin by drawing whatever type of energy you will be using into yourself. The conjuring of the column using the "Descendat Columba, Ascendat Serpens" formula that was given in Chapter 2 is one way to accomplish this and draw upon energy in general. Elemental pore breathing, wherein the body is seen as empty and an elemental force is drawn in through the pores of the body, was covered in the section on shields (page 51), and can be used here as well. Earth may be chosen for providing protection, Water for smoothing over tense situations and engendering understanding, and so forth for Fire and Air.

The forces of the planets can be breathed into the body as well by performing the ritual during the proper planetary day and hour while concentrating on the colors and symbols of the planet.[11] Sexual energy can be built up and used for this purpose as well, but is a bit more complex and isn't the best to use for protective purposes. A full description of this technique will have to wait for another book.

When the body is filled with force, you should set your gaze upon the space set aside for the spirit to manifest within. You must now eject the force through your navel and see it shoot from you and form a cloud in front of you. Through force of will, command the cloud of energy to take the shape that you have determined ahead of time. The more detail you put into this, the better the spirit will manifest. If you are very talented at visualizing, you can even go so far as to imagine the energy taking the form of microscopic versions of the spirit's sigil, which then form the cells of the being and eventually coalesce into the form of the servitor. If you have limited powers of visualization, you must work to the best of your ability.

Once you see the spirit in front of you, it is time to cut the connection, name it, and give it its orders. A simple "I name you ____; you are _____" will suffice for the naming. Its orders should likewise be succinct and to the point. If the spirit is meant for temporary use, you must give it an order to dissipate at a future time whether it has accomplished its task or not. It is better to use an astronomical event to mark time with spirits than it is to use a calendar date. The next equinox, the new moon, or when the Sun moves into a new sign are all examples that would work. If you are planning to keep the servitor around permanently, you should be vigilant in feeding it energy and reinforcing its programming at regular intervals.

After you have issued it orders, command it to depart and carry them out. If you are binding the spirit to an object, you can see the servitor sink into the object. If you are not binding it, then simply see the servitor fly off to carry out its mission.

The potential uses of servitors and the methods of their construction are endless, and the reason I have a ritual outline instead of a script is that this form of magick is so wonderfully imaginative that everyone should develop their own techniques. The benefit of using a servitor as opposed to a preexisting entity lies in its complete obedience to your will. You are its creator and master. This is also its flaw, as a preexisting spirit can occasionally find ways to assist you that you would never even think of.

In either case, the use of spirits for defense is often necessary in the event of a full-blown magickal attack. Amulets and banishing rituals are great at preventing harm, but can eventually be circumvented by a cunning-enough technique. Spirits, artificial or not, are often used in launching attacks because of their ability to adapt to defenses and get past them.

If you think that an artificial spirit has been sent against you by someone else, you can combat it in a number of ways. Some artificial spirits are nothing more than thought-forms projected by a creator without any other type of energy put into them at all. In this case you can destroy them by thinking them away. It's that simple—just imagine them being obliterated; from mind they came and by mind they go. If you banish and visualize them away, yet they resist, you have got another problem.

In the case of an artificial elemental you can fight it off or destroy it by trapping it in a triangle, such as the Hekatean spirit trap, and attacking it with the opposing element and associated weapons. One can also begin to feed it the element that it is made out of, thus making it stronger but infusing it with your will in an attempt to usurp control. This is slightly more dangerous, but has its advantages. If you are successful in taking over an artificial spirit, it is a powerful magickal link to a potentially unknown attacker. It's difficult and should be attempted only by experienced practitioners, but may prove to be easier than getting hair and fingernail clippings.

In fact, there are plenty of cases where spirits that were sent to attack someone were usurped by the victim and turned upon the attacker. This is done either through making greater offerings to the spirit, binding the spirit as you would in an exorcism, or appealing to the spirit's nature. I have been told of instances in Haiti where a bokor (sorcerer) sent one of the barons, Lwa, who is associated with death and the graveyard, amongst other things, against another bokor. The targeted sorcerer made prayers to the same baron, and basically left it up to the baron to decide who was justified in his case. In the end it was the first bokor, the one who initiated the attack, who was taken to the grave.

This technique of forcing a spirit to choose between two victims in the hopes that the unjustified person will be killed is also seen in the Pulsa Dinura, or Lashes of Fire curse, which was mentioned in an earlier chapter. This curse is performed in a cemetery and invokes the angel of death, asking him to kill a named victim or kill the person performing the curse. It is up to the angel to decide who deserves death. The curse was used on October 6, 1995, by the Israeli politician Avigdor Eskin against Yitzhak Rabin in response to the Oslo Accords. Rabin was assassinated within the month. More recently, the curse was used against Ariel Sharon, who slipped into a coma shortly afterward and died in 2014.[12]

Using such techniques is obviously dangerous and advanced work, but I mention them for the sake of completeness. It is up to you to decide what you are ready to use and when. In general, you will be better served by using the defensive techniques already mentioned and the methods of reversal and counter-magick that I will teach in the next chapter.

NEW EDITION COMMENTARY

One of the coolest things about being the author of a book is getting to hear about, and occasionally see, people putting the book to good use. Over the years I have been blown away with how many people have made the Apoxias bottle. The items for this bottle are not the easiest to come by, and I am thrilled at the dedication that so many readers have taken in either gathering the formula as written, or taking great care in substitutions.

Aconite was included as an ingredient for the bottle in the original book and is the only substantial change that I have made in the body of the book itself. It now lists dandelion instead. When I made my spirit house, I wore gloves and handled the aconite with care. It was going into a bottle that was never going to be opened again, after all, so the danger was small. Aconite is deadly, but its inclusion has as much to do with being sacred to Hekate and to the underworld as anything else. There is a legend that states aconite started to spring up from places where Cerberus, the three-headed guardian of Hades, drooled. Dandelion is also sacred to Hekate and is related to the underworld because the roots extend downward in equal length to the flower above ground. Thus I have changed the ingredient aconite to dandelion.

The other ingredient people have had issue finding is blackthorn, as it's not readily available in the States. I got mine from England, but if you really cannot get any blackthorn you can choose another, more local, thorny substitution.

Whenever making any kind of substitution in magick you need to hold two seemingly contradictory ideas in mind at the same time:

PROTECTION & REVERSAL MAGICK

1. Absolutely everything matters. It's there for a reason, and changing what goes in will change what comes out.

2. Very few things are necessary. Just because a substitution or omission changes what you get, that does not necessarily make it worse. It might be worse, or it might just be different, or it might even be an improvement.

I explain this as "The Grilled Cheese Rule." I was taught to make grilled cheese with butter on the outside of the bread and three kinds of cheese on the inside. If, however you don't have butter, you can make a grilled cheese with mayonnaise. It will be different, but not necessarily worse. Same with the cheeses. If you can't use cheddar for sharpness, Swiss for stringiness, and American for meltiness, you can omit one or use different cheeses entirely. It will still be grilled cheese, but it will also be different.

Of course, when you play this out to extremes, you can omit or substitute so much that it really is no longer the same thing at all. Using fried chicken instead of cheese might tickle your fancy, but it ain't grilled cheese. In the formula above if you do change every ingredient and change the seal of the spirit, it stops being the Apoxias bottle. It might be decent magick, but it's not this magick.

Get it?

Chapter 7

REVERSALS AND
COUNTER-MAGICK

If you are vigilant in your banishings, use protective amulets, and have strong guardians, even if someone were to lay a curse directly on you, it is likely that you would probably not even notice. The entire attack will roll off you or be sent back to the sender automatically. There can be times, however, when the normal defenses do not hold, and a more active position will need to be assumed to ensure the well-being of you and your loved ones. Thus far we have dealt only with strictly pacifying, protective, and preventative measures. Under the majority of circumstances, these will be all that is needed. Unfortunately, in some cases, an obsessive enemy will show no sign of stopping his or her harassment, and you will need to resort to more heavy-handed methods to ensure a successful defense. For this reason, it is important to master the techniques of reversal and counter-magick.

There is a well-known axiom that has entered Wicca known as the Law of Three. This law is typically interpreted as a sort of amplified karma and states that any harm done by the witch will come back upon her three times over. According to some of my contacts in the traditional craft, the original meaning of the Law of Three is a bit different. The idea was that if a witch is harmed or cursed that she or he should *send it back to the offender three times over.* This ensures that the enemy, should she survive the triple reversal, not attempt the same foolishness again. As this book is a primer on defense only, I will not be concentrating on sending things back "three times over." It is, however, sometimes a good idea to reverse an attack upon the attacker, forcing her to fall into a trap of her own making.

IDENTIFYING YOUR ATTACKER

Though it's not always necessary, it is beneficial if you know who it is that you are reversing a curse back upon. Unfortunately, this is not always possible. While some less-adept sorcerers rely on the psychological power of someone knowing that he or she has been cursed as part of the curse itself, a truly powerful witch will not reveal his identity, allowing the curse to work in secret. If your enemy has not shown his hand by pointing dramatically and pronouncing a curse verbally, he may have left evidence in the form of physical objects used to deliver the curse to you. Powders such as Goofer Dust and Graveyard Dust are common, as are a host of other condition powders such as Bend Over, Crossing, Commanding, and Black Arts. These powders are usually laid in a place where you will come into contact with them or step on them, such as on the doorstep, in the car, or even on a paper that is mailed to you. Apart from powders, items such as gris-gris bags, jack balls, and paper talismans can also be placed in or around your home or office to deliver the power to you. If any of these or other suspect items are found, they can be gathered and used to hone your reversal spells on the correct sender.

If there are no items that you can find, perhaps the offender has collected something of yours to use as a link. Think about people whom you have had as guests, who may have used your bathroom recently where they could have gotten some hair from your brush or nail clippings from the wastebasket. Think about anyone who had access to your office or your living space. Also think about people who have offered you food or gifts, taking a page out of the Trojan army playbook: many types of curses can be delivered through food, and gifts can be dressed and consecrated to convey curses. Next, ask yourself if any of these people would have reason to harm you for any reason. Lastly, assess whether they would have the ability and knowledge to place a curse themselves and, if not, whether they would pay someone to do it on their behalf. There shouldn't be a lot of candidates who fit the bill. If there are, then I would suggest that you have bigger problems than just this one curse.

Whether you can come up with suspects using these methods, or if you just think you know who did it, you should ALWAYS do a divination before attempting a reversal geared at sending a curse back to a specific person. If you pick the wrong person, it is likely that he won't feel the effect of the reversal, but he could pick up some bad energy sent his way in the process. It is also possible that what you think is a curse is actually crossed conditions brought on by magickal missteps or inadvertently broken oaths. If you attempt to reverse this back upon the sender, you will be sending it back upon yourself; and, like two mirrors being placed face to face, the reflection will go on forever, making the problem worse and worse.

A good method for divining the identity of an attacker is to write the names of the suspects on a piece of paper, adding one additional name of "unknown" in the event that the real culprit is not on your list. Place the pendulum (I use a lodestone pendulum suspended by my own clipped hair, but a store-bought pendulum will work fine) over the first name and ask if that person is the one who placed the curse on you. There is not space here to give an extensive teaching on the use of pendulums, but one should be able to clear one's mind, connect with the divine, and then ask if that name is the name of the one who cursed you. If it is, then the pendulum should swing wildly. Other methods such as drawing cards or runes for each name are equally valid. If you find that you are too scattered to do an effective divination (you are potentially under a hex, after all) or if you are too emotionally invested to get an objective answer, a third party should be brought in to do the divining on your behalf.

Whatever the preferred method, you should rely on divination to confirm your suspicions and to see what outcome will be had. I cannot stress this enough. It may be that your reversal will do more harm than good. Early in my magickal career I was the target of a nasty jinx that caused me some minor headaches and broken knick-knacks due to fumbled hands. After searching for curse material, I found a sigil on paper under one of the floor mats in my car. I used the paper as a link to reverse the jinx back upon the sender by burning a candle upside down, which is described on pages 142–143. A week or so later, it came to my attention that a girlfriend I parted on not-so-good terms with got into a car accident and was in the hospital with some serious injuries. She wasn't a serious practitioner, but after confronting her with the sigil, she admitted that she had picked up a book and decided to lay a jinx on me to show that I wasn't such a good magician. As it happens, most of her jinx was counteracted by my daily rituals and protection measures, measures that she was not taking because she was only a casual practitioner. She received the full force of the jinx she meant to place on me, and because she had no magickal protection, it was quite destructive. This was a case where, if I had known the outcome, I would have not reversed the jinx because I would not want to cause that kind of harm to someone I knew, even if they did do something against me out of anger.

REVERSAL SPELLS

Tangled in the Devil's Shoestrings

After deciding whether or not to reverse the spell, and, if possible, divining the identity of the culprit, you are ready to do the actual reversal. If you believe that the curse centers on your home, an excellent method for reversing the spell is to get some dirt from the offender's home, nine pieces of devil's shoestring, and a jar. Begin the spell by bringing to mind the jinx that has been placed upon you. Try as best you can to tap into that force set against you, to get a psychic "feel" for its frequency. Take up a piece of devil's shoestring in your right hand and trace a cross in the air in front of you, feeling the root gather up the energy of the spell. As you make the vertical arm of the cross, say, "I am not in power of thine." When making the horizontal arm of the cross, say, "Thou art in power of mine." Do this nine times, once with each piece of devil's shoestring. Take all nine pieces of devil's shoestring and place them in a jar with the dirt from your enemy's house, some red and black pepper, and some poppy seeds, intermingling them all together. Go back to the culprit's house and, as you sprinkle the mix in their yard or on their porch, say:

What malice you have aimed at me
shall now be returned unto thee
By word and will, so shall it be.

Walk away from the home without looking back.

This ritual quite literally binds the curse up, removing it from your sphere, and delivers it back upon the sender in one neat package. When you return home you should banish well, cleanse your house, and fortify whatever protections you have in place.

Upside-Down Candle Reversal Spell

The practice of burning candles "upside down" is a popular technique often used in cursing, but can also be used to reverse a curse back upon the sender. You will need a black candle, a pot of dirt, and some powdered crab shells. Take the black candle, light it, and place it in a candleholder. As in the previous spell, attempt to mentally tap into the frequency of the powers that have been set against you while concentrating on the candle. This candle now represents the original curse. When your mind has firmly grasped onto the power of the curse, pull the candle up from its holder and snuff it out in the pot of dirt and crab shells. The spell will work without the crab shells, but they represent reversal because they walk backwards, and so make an extra element. With your mind intent on reversing the curse back upon the sender, bite the bottom of the candle off, revealing the wick. Light the candle at the end that you bit off and place the candle back in its holder. As you do so, give it the following charge:

Thy Artifice has been reversed
Thy Curse has been returned
By Force and Fire and Cunning Will
Be thou the victim of thine own ill.

All of these actions should be done in an emotional state of justified anger, particularly the snuffing and the biting. Allow the candle to burn all the way down. At the end you can gather up the wax and the dirt and either deposit them at your enemy's house or throw them into moving water.

Double-Action Reversal Candles

Another candle spell to reverse a jinx uses a special candle, sometimes called a Double-Action Reversal Candle. This candle is white on the top, signifying the clearing of the curse from your life, and black on the bottom to send the curse back upon the sender. The way that this is used is to dress the candle with reversing oil. Chances are you can purchase condition oils such as this one anywhere that you can buy one of these candles, but if you want to make your own, you can soak dill, rue, and devil's shoestring in a good carrier oil such as almond oil or virgin olive oil. Hold the candle horizontally with the bottom facing you and rub the oil from the bottom to the top, away from your body. As you do this, concentrate on reversing the curse or crossed condition back from where it came.

If you know the identity of the target, you should get a photo or some other object link and place it underneath the candle. If you don't know the identity of the target, then simply place a paper under the candle addressed to "those who do me harm." Place a drop of reversing oil on each of the four corners and in the center of the paper or photo.

Light the candle and pray:
Shadow, hear my call to thee
Pitiful hate-filled enemy
Be malignant if you will
For I am more malignant still.

I turn you over to Hekate
To send the curse back to thee
Damning you as the wax burns down
Committing your power to the ground.

Let the candle burn all the way down, then collect the wax and the personal items and bury them near a three-way crossroads. If you can't do this at a three-way crossroads, you can do it at a graveyard (but not on a grave, which would be overkill). The idea is that you are sealing the spell by delivering it to Hekate Chthonos, who dwells in the underworld.

Spitting Back a Jinx

The herb galangal, known to rootworkers as "Little John," is most famous for its use in influencing court cases. A defendant would chew some Little John and then spit it out in the court to influence things in his favor. What is not as well known is that the same spell can also be used for turning back jinxes. Once again, attempt to mentally "tune in" to the frequency of the curse. Then, put pieces of galangal root in your mouth and chew. As you chew, think about how angry you are at the harm that has been done to you and how justified you are in sending it back to the source. Enflame yourself in these thoughts of justice and, at the climax, spit the root out with force in the direction of your enemy. If you can perform this reversal where the one who originated the curse actually lives, that is even better. If you are unable to divine the source of the jinx, then spit the root toward the west. When you are finished, walk home and don't look back. Perform a banishing ritual when you get home.

The Lamp of Reversal

The lamp of reversal is burned to drive back any ill set against you. To make the lamp, hollow out half a coconut and fill it with vegetable oil. In the oil place nine needles, nine pins, nine nails, and nine pieces of devil's shoestring, and some dill, salt, and rue. Float a wick in a piece of cork (special wick kits can be bought at most good botanicas) and light it while making the following invocation:

Nails, shoestring, rue, salt, and dill
Hinder my enemies of their will
As they would do ill unto me
Hold them to their own agony
Hear my will addressed to thee
By word and will, so shall it be

This lamp is best burned outside, but if you don't have a yard, you can place it in the window. Burn the lamp every Friday for seven weeks. Be careful to make sure there is enough oil in the lamp at all times. Add more as needed.

The Mirror Cage

We have already touched upon mirrors in the section on protecting the home. For obvious reasons, the mirror is a classic tool for reversing spells back upon their sender. Another way to use a mirror in spell reversal is to get a small box (I use ones shaped as coffins, which can be purchased around Halloween, but any box with a lid will do) and line the inside with shards of mirror, making sure to cover as much surface as possible. Make a poppet to symbolize your enemy—this can be a simple effigy made from wax (even a wax figure candle of the appropriate gender will do) or a fabric doll stuffed with Spanish moss and appropriate herbs. If you have an article that was used in the original bewitchment, such as a powder or conjure hand, or if you have a personal link to the target, such as hair or cloth, then you should work it into the doll; if not, include a name paper in the doll or carve the name of the target onto the doll. If you do not know the name of the offending sorcerer, simply write, "The one who works against me."

> Hold the doll in your left hand and with your right hand trace
>   a cross over the doll. As you trace the vertical arm of the
>   cross, say, "I baptize thee (name of target)." If you don't
>   know the name of the target, you can substitute the
>   word *shadow*. As you make the horizontal arm of the
>   cross, say, "Thou art in my power."
> Place the doll into the box that has been lined with mirrors
>   and say the following:
> (Name of target), for your own sake
> I pray you no more trouble make
> For to torment me for your own gain
> Will only bring you greater pain
> For I am a child of Hekate
> And she is mightier than thee
> From this hour forth all ill intent
> Shall back upon thy head be sent
> In the name of Neboutosaoaleth, Ereshkigal, and Aktiophis
> And by my own word and will
> Thou shall be thine own victim.

After you have said the charm and closed the box, you should place it in a safe place on your altar or bury it somewhere, such as at a crossroads. This spell will have the effect of mirroring anything that the offending warlock does back upon himself, be it good or ill.

Before moving on from reversals, I would like to say that while it may be the case that justice is best served by reversing harm back upon the sender, sometimes this will only cause the sender to resort to more volatile measures against you, followed by you resorting to stronger measures to repel them. This is, of course, how wars begin, and like mundane wars, the gain is often not worth the cost. Becoming obsessed with reversing curses often leads to sending them yourself and can lead to an obsessive life. Like that of Heathcliff of *Wuthering Heights*, who returned only such agonies as he himself received, your whole life can get sucked into a web of justified vengeance. This is, to my mind, not a good way to live life or an effective way to deal with interlopers, and so I offer you counter-magick techniques aimed at ridding yourself of your enemy.

COUNTER-MAGICK

We will define counter-magick as magick that is done to counteract an attack, but is not a direct protection from, or reversal of, that attack. The full range of possibilities is wide indeed and could even include our own offensive curses. However, because this is a book geared toward protection, and there are more than enough ways to deal with these situations without generating our own offensive magick, I will forgo teaching anything meant to outright harm an enemy. We will be focusing on binding, confusing, and expelling— all techniques that are used to get an enemy to stop focusing on causing harm without going ahead and causing harm ourselves.

Because counter-magick techniques all focus on removing us from an enemy's environment or the enemy from ours, they are the most useful techniques for dealing with nonmagickal dangers. If someone is threatening your life or the lives of your loved ones with physical violence, shields and amulets may have some effect, but eventually you will need to remove that person from your life to be safe.

Just as I do not recommend trying to deal with medical or psychological problems without consulting professionals in those fields first, counter-magick should not take the place of law enforcement professionals when dealing with a dangerous person. If someone has threatened your life or the lives of the people you love, I think you have every right to use the following methods of binding, expelling, confusing, and silencing against him, but you will be doing yourself a disservice if you don't contact the authorities. Indeed, it is often *through* the agency of the authorities that the binding or expelling takes effect in these cases.

Whether the danger you face is mundane or spiritual, it is through counter-magick that very persistent problems can be laid to rest and ongoing wars settled.

Binding and Influencing

Bindings are used to stop someone from doing a particular thing or to heavily influence someone towards doing something, in our case leaving us and our loved ones or clients alone.

Bend Over Powder

Just as powders such as Goofer Dust are used in jinxing and cursing, and other powders such as red brick dust are used for protection, there are also powders used in counter-magick. A good one for binding is the famous Bend Over Powder, which is made with licorice root, calamus root, and High John the Conqueror ground into a powder and mixed with a base powder such as talcum. The powder is then used by laying it where the target will step on or touch it. If laying the powder on the ground to "send through the feet," it is done while walking backwards and is often laid in a five-spot pattern such as you would find on dice. If not, then you can keep the powder in your pocket and deliver it by a handshake directly. Another time-honored way to deliver a powder is to sprinkle some on a letter and mail it to the target, making sure that only an undetectable amount is left—we don't want to get arrested for causing an anthrax scare.

This powder can be especially effective if you are confronting the enemy face-to-face to work out differences. If used in this manner, you can coat your hand with the dust or make sure that he or she comes into contact with the dust at some point during the conversation. Once he does, you should attempt to focus your gaze on your enemy's forehead between the eyebrows. If you can focus your will like a laser beam on this point, you will be able to dominate the conversation and affect the mind of the target. At the very least, by using your gaze in this way, any magickal attempts to do the same to you will be returned or counteracted.

Tanglefoot Charm

The Tanglefoot Charm is an old European spell of binding using a cord. It can be used to stop someone from doing any one particular thing. That thing could be a curse or other type of harassment, but also could be something else such as going to work. Even in purely altruistic cases, you must remember that magick manifests in natural

ways, and you must be willing to accept the consequences of
your actions.

   A few years back, a friend of mine was being stalked and came to
me for help. Using a letter that the stalker had written to her as a link,
I used the Tanglefoot Charm to bind him from stalking her. For a week
and a half there was no change. He would sit outside her house at
night and call constantly. I thought perhaps that the spell didn't work,
and I would have to move to something stronger. Then one night my
friend heard a crash outside her bedroom window. When she looked
outside, she saw a ladder on the ground and her stalker splayed over
the fence. He had broken both of his legs and suffered other small
injuries. This was also enough for her to press charges. He stalked her
no more. I was more than happy to accept the responsibility for that,
but some would not be. I again urge the reader to divine the outcome
of your work to the best of your ability.

   To work the Tanglefoot Charm you will need some link to the target that can be tied into red cord. Taking the red cord in the left hand,
concentrate on the thing that you wish your enemy not to do any-
more and tie nine knots in the cord, starting at the outer edges and
moving in like this: 1-3-5-7-9-8-6-4-2. As you do so, say the following
incantation with each knot:

   (Name of target), I conjure thee
   By the power of Earth thou art tangled
   By the power of rock thou art bound
   By the power of clay thou art chained
   Held in place by the weight of the ground

   Work the personal item of the target into the ninth knot. When
you have completed this, go to a crossroads and bury the cord there.
Saying the following:

(Name of target), I bury your power (to do harm to me, or
    whatever the binding is for)
Twisted and tangled
Chained and bound
I lay thee to rest
Committed to ground.

Walk away from the site and do not look back.

Graveyard Binding

Another excellent binding uses the grave of a soldier or police officer.
Take a material link of the harm doer such as a photo or cloth, and
wrap it up with nine pieces of devil's shoestring or some knot weed. If
you have some lead, wrap it in lead (the metal of Saturn). If not, you
can wrap it up in aluminum foil, shiny side in. Take it to the grave of
the loved one, relative, or soldier, and make an offering of whiskey
or a dime as if you were collecting graveyard dust. Dig a shallow hole
over where you suppose the right hand is located and bury the charm
there.

It is best to use your own words for this spell, speaking directly to
the spirit in the grave, but it should go something like this:

(Name of spirit in the grave), I come to you to ask for your
    help
(Name of enemy) has caused me harm and will not leave me
    alone
I give them to you. Keep them away from me until I return
    for them.
Accept my payment and do this for me, I pray.

Leave the gravesite and never return. Obviously, if this is a grave you visit often, for magickal or sentimental reasons, it is *not* a good grave to use. You should make sure it is a grave that you will never visit again.

To Stop Talk about You

Figure 7.1 Seal of Saturn

The following spell is said to bind the enemy from even talking about you. Take a beef tongue and wrap up your links to the enemy in a paper with the seal of Saturn upon it covering the target's name:

You can dress the sigil paper with oils and powders of binding as you choose.

Slice open the beef tongue and place the paper and seal inside, then sew it back up. Place the tongue in the back of your freezer and say the following:

Ereshigal, Nocticula, Hekate
Grow forth and witness my rite!
Seize my enemy's tongue!
May not even his words exist! Sigy! Sigy! Sigy!
So shall it be!

Another way to silence an enemy (or a noisy neighbor, for that matter) is a simple gris-gris bag made from licorice root, slippery elm, and adder's-tongue. Wrap it up in a black bag and plant the bag under the person's doorstep or somewhere in their yard or house.

CONFUSION

When binding is not possible, another way to remove an enemy working against you without bringing him or her into direct harm is rites of confusion. Some see this as a type of jinx in and of itself, but confusion spells have been used in hoodoo and witchcraft as protection for many, many years. When faced with an obsessive enemy who will not give up after protection and reversal rites have been worked, a bit of confusion can be a tame but effective way to deal with that enemy.

Confusion Powder

This powder is used in the same way as the other powders and is, to my mind, one of the best ways to deliver this type of spell. A couple of years ago I had a client who was in danger of losing his business because the owner of a restaurant chain wanted the space he was in. This person was also spreading rumors about my client and causing him all kinds of hassle with the town in an effort to get him to move. To make matters worse, my friend believed that one of the restaurant owner's family members was a witch and was working against the store magickally. I happened to know from prior experience that his suspicions about this were correct, and after several readings decided that a confusion spell was the best option. I surrounded the restaurant with Confusion Powder on a new moon and prayed to Hekate as I did so. I spread some on the doormats as well. I soon began to hear complaints about the restaurant, and it was not long after that it was temporarily closed for health violations. Soon thereafter the financial backer who was going to help him buy my friend's store fell through.

This ritual went almost exactly as I planned, and I was happy with the results. However, I must stress that you should always do a divination to get an idea of what your results will be. I was more than prepared to accept responsibility for this person to lose money by having his restaurant temporarily closed and for him to suffer other minor problems, but if the reading had indicated people getting seriously hurt by my spell, I would have used something else. Confusion spells are tricky in this way, as confusion can be the cause of vehicular accidents and all kinds of more serious issues. I am not here to preach to you, only to tell you that you need to be responsible for your actions.

Confusion Powder is made with poppy seeds, twitch grass, and black mustard seeds added to a powder base such as talcum. Some people color their powders, and if you do, the appropriate color would be red. If you want to cause arguments and infighting as well as confusion amongst your enemies, add in black and red pepper. The same recipe could be used to make not only a powder, but also an oil or incense. The clever witch will be able to employ all three, such as in the following spell.

A Confusion Doll

If there is someone in your life who is perpetually causing you problems and sending psychic attacks your way, but whom you can't cut ties with completely, such as a family member, it may be a good idea to make a Confusion Doll of that person that you can activate at will. To make the doll, get the best personal link you can. Make a frame from two pieces of wood tied together as a cross. You can make the body of the doll from the target's clothing; failing that, use red cloth and make a body around the cross using a combination of Spanish moss and twitch grass wrapped in the cloth. You can make a head for the doll out of clay or use the head of an actual doll. If using clay, work poppy and black mustard seeds into the clay before making the head. If using an actual doll's head, stuff it with the seeds.

With your right hand, trace a cross over the doll. As you make the vertical bar, say, "I name thee (name of target)." As you make the horizontal bar, say, "Thou art (name of target)."

Light some Confusion Incense either purchased from a store or made from all the herbs mentioned so far, and hold the doll over the smoke with your left hand. As you hold the doll over the smoke, bring to mind all the harm that the target has done to you in the past. Enflame yourself with righteous rage and desire for justice. Allow this to flow into the doll as you say:

Inimicus Carpo!
Fazed and flustered
Vexed and addled
Lost in the smoke of delusion
I hold thee firm
Bewildered and bound
Cast into confusion
By word and will addressed to thee

Confusion to (name of target) be!

Expelling

The last type of counter-magick that I want to cover is that of expelling, more commonly known in rootworking as "hot-footing." This type of magick is aimed at getting a person to leave your environment totally. Usually you are expelling the person either from a home, from a job, or from a town. As with the other types of counter-magick, we will begin with a powder.

Hot-Foot Powder

Generally speaking, anything hot or stinging can be used in Hot-Foot Powder. My favorite recipe for the powder is red and black pepper, crushed hornets or red ants, sulfur, poppy seeds, and witch's salt (salt that has been blackened with soot). This powder is used in a similar way as the others and is particularly potent if it can be "sent through the foot" by having them walk on it or by putting it in their shoes. One of my favorite ways to use this is to sprinkle it on the doorstep or office of the target, then drop a little bit at each crossroads leading out of town, praying for the person to move each time you drop it.

One sorcerer I know uses the entire Catholic Rite of Exorcism when doing rites like this, but I like the following incantation:

> By the Fire of Azazel!
> I send thee to the Desert!
> Barra! Edin Na Zu!
> Barra! Edin Na Zu!
> Barra! Edin Na Zu![1]

Another Method of Sending through the Feet

If you can't get the person to walk on it, another traditional way to send through the foot is to "pick up" the footprint of the target. A close friend of mine was having issues with a coworker a couple years back and reported to me that he was having a strange run of bad headaches and worse luck. He confided to me that the coworker he was having trouble with practiced magick, and he thought it was probable that he was putting a jinx on him and wanted my help. Readings indicated that he was correct, and I used a reversal spell to turn magick back. It seemed to work for a while, but then the attack was renewed. We did this one more time, but the same thing happened. It became apparent that we needed to separate them entirely. I had my friend watch where his target walked when leaving the office. I instructed him to quietly pick up some dirt from one of his footprints, which he did. He brought the dirt back to me and I mixed in red and black pepper, sulfur, and some crushed hornets. I bottled the whole thing up in a jar and tossed the jar into some running water. As I did, I said:

> By Acheron, by Cocytus
> By Phlegethon, Styx, and Lethe
> I cast thee out!
> May not even the memory
> Of your name remain!
> By the Acheron,
> By the Cocytus
> By the Phlegethon, Styx, and Lethe[2]
> Begone! Begone! Begone!

Shortly after this spell was cast, the target found a better-paying job and moved on. It worked out to be the best for everyone. In fact, if you are worried about causing someone harm, you can add herbs of blessing, such as angelica, to the Expelling Powder mix to help the target move on to better circumstances.

An interesting variant of this type of spell was recorded by the priest and anthropologist Harry Middleton Hyatt. Rather than bottling up the foot track and casting it into a river, his informant told of putting the dirt and the hot-foot materials into a hollowed-out shotgun shell and shooting it off into the distance, while praying to Jesus for the person to be removed from your life! I haven't ever tried this method, but the drama alone would be powerful.

Spirits in Counter-Magick

Spirits can be used in counter-magick as well. Many of the guardian spirits from various traditions also function in this capacity. In Tibet, for instance, a form of the Goddess Tara known as Osel Chenma rides upon a pig and carries a needle and thread that she uses to sew up the eyes and ears of enemies. Many angels and spirits from the grimoires can also be summoned for binding and expelling people from your life, and you can follow the instructions in those texts to summon them. In particular, I have used Zazel, the spirit of Saturn from Agrippa's Three Books of Occult Philosophy, in binding with excellent results.

The guardian spirit Apoxias, whose summoning we covered in the previous chapter, can also be used in counter-magick and excels at binding, confusing, and expelling. To use him in this way, you should set up an altar with his bottle in front of you. Feed the bottle with energy and chant the summoning mantra IO APOX-IAS IO HO. When you feel that you have gotten his attention, you should ask him to bind, confuse, or expel from your life the person or spirit who is harassing you. If you want to make sure that no harm is brought to the target, then you should say so. In cases where your life is in danger, you may choose to let Apoxias act as he will. As always, you must take responsibility for your own actions. If you have a link to the target, you should fold it up in a paper, taking care to fold the paper away from you as you do it. Draw the sigil of Apoxias on the paper and place the bottle on top of it. If the personal link is too bulky to fit under the bottle, then place it in front of the bottle instead.

PROTECTION & REVERSAL MAGICK

Artificial Elementals in Counter-Magick

I have already talked a bit about artificial elementals in the chapter on guardians. They can also be put to great use in the field of counter-magick, but instead of Earth and Water, we focus on the elements of Air for confusion and Fire for expelling. To recap, an artificial elemental is a spirit form created by the magician and imbued with power from one or more of the four elements and given temporary artificial consciousness through the sorcerer's will.

The first thing that you will need is a name and a statement of purpose. Because I have already given the general form of how to create an artificial spirit in the previous chapter, it may be helpful to use an example from real life. An occult group that I belonged to in Philadelphia had admitted a person that soon proved to be dangerous in both magickal and mundane ways. Though he didn't outright attack anyone in the group, several people felt threatened, and it was clear that some of his activities were criminal, to say the least. A friend and I decided to do an expelling rite and we created an artificial Fire elemental to do so. Because the element was Fire, the planet associated with what we wanted was Mars, so we took those words, Fire and Mars, and made the name RAMSIEF. Combining those letters into a sigil we came up with Figure 7.2 on p. 160.

Bringing in influence from the zodiac sign Aries, we decided that Ramsief would appear as a ram-headed, very large, red humanoid with six arms, each of which held a flaming axe. Another, and perhaps better, method we could have used for all this would be to make an invocation to the element Fire and the planet Mars and ask for inspiration. We might have received a vision of the elemental, name, and seal either in meditation or dream. In this case, though, we decided to construct it entirely ourselves.

Figure 7.2 Sigil of Ramsief

After opening a circle and invoking the watchtowers in our typical fashion, we marked out a triangle on the altar and began to pore breathe the element Fire, which has the qualities of heat, dryness, and expansion. Once we had gathered a sufficient amount of Fire element in our bodies, we projected it out into the triangle, first seeing it gather as cloud of flames, then seeing that take the shape of Ramsief. Once the figure was formed and could be "seen" by both my partner and me, we drew our wands (the tool associated with Fire in our tradition) and, pointing at Ramsief, addressed it thus:

> By the Lords of the Southern Gate
> By the White ones of the Noontide Hour
> By the Sovereign Spirits of Notus
> And by All the Djinn of the Desert I name thee Ramsief,
> Thou art Ramsief.
> Go forth and expel (name of target) from this city.
> Remove him from our midst
> Accomplish this within the space of three moons.
> On the Third Full Moon
> Whether you have accomplished your task or not
> Dissipate back into the element of Fire
> And seek the peace of oblivion
> Heed my words and do my will
> Fiat! Fiat! Fiat!

In all cases of reversal and counter-magick, you should always remember to do a divination, and be sure that you really are under spiritual attack from another human being and not experiencing crossed conditions stemming from your own missteps or retribution from spirits of one kind or another.

You should attempt as much as possible to see the outcome of your spells because you must take responsibility for that outcome. Unless you have a professional magickal practice of some kind, it is likely that you will need these lessons only two or three times during your entire life. People who find themselves constantly embroiled in psychic showdowns are generally not under real attack and are just using the occult to draw some drama into an otherwise dull existence.

If you do find yourself the target of magickal attacks very often, I would suggest that asking yourself why and making changes in your friends and lifestyle will serve you better than all the reversals and counter-magick in the world. That being said, magickal attacks *do* occur, and mastering the techniques in this chapter can help preserve your health and well-being in tight situations.

NEW EDITION COMMENTARY

The reversals and counter-magick in this chapter are solid. I am happy with them. The only thing I want to address is the idea of identifying the attacker. Magickal traditions the world over would have to rely on divination to tell if someone is attacking you, and that is what I went with in the book. I want to stress this now: If you are planning a targeted counterattack, curse, or retaliation, *divination is not enough*.

Divination is one point of data. Actionable intelligence is made up of many different types of data that corroborate each other. As I said in the new introduction, the number of people that I don't even know, who think I have cursed them because someone divined it, has been kind of shocking for me. It is clear to me that many readers will choose to confirm the suspicions of a client for the sake of drama, or to sell them counter-magick, or just to avoid the discomfort that comes from telling someone that they are wrong.

A few times now someone has come to me after visiting three or four different readers. The readers each confirmed a curse, but each identified a different culprit. Rather than questioning the readings, the client assumes that all three parties are actively cursing them! So let me say here: No, your mom, your ex, and that person you had a fight with online are not all burning candles against you. Probably none of them are. You may laugh, but these are real examples.

I use divination and I hope you do too, but sometimes, when there is little chance of verifiable information contradicting a reading, people put a little too much faith in it. Would you invest your life savings based on only a divination? Probably not. You would treat it as one point of data and do other kinds of research. Please treat identifying an enemy you are going to strike at with the same level of care. If you don't know with reasonable certainty who is working against you, identify "my enemy" or "the person working against me" in your counter-magick. Most of the time it works just as well, and you might be surprised at the person who suddenly takes ill or has to suddenly leave.

Chapter 8

HEALING AND RECOVERY

Whatever the particular circumstances of your situation, when the dust settles and all the methods of attack and defense have been exhausted, it is time to clean up the mess and get back to business as usual. After you reaffirm your regular defenses and repair any cracks in the fortress, you will need to tend to your wounds. The residual effects of magickal attack can linger like an attack in and of themselves. These problems range from physical symptoms, such as aches and pains, to psychological symptoms, such as an inability to sleep, depression, and unexplainable anxiety. Even more probable are outward conditions, such as runs of bad luck and a feeling of being out of step with time.

In all cases, occult treatment should not replace medical treatment. Medical doctors, therapists, and psychologists should be consulted when appropriate. It is also beneficial to seek the help of professional psychic healers from whatever tradition you come from, be it a Reiki practitioner or the local shaman.

The first and best way to make reparations after an attack is prayer and acts of devotion. Thank the gods and the spirits for taking care of you in your hour of need. If you worship no gods, then direct your devotion to the enlightened ones who have gone before you and serve as guides on the path. Direct it to the universe itself. It is not my place to tell you how to pray or what to pray to, but I do want to stress the awesome potential of energized prayer. I again refer you to the advice of Israel Regardie, who said to "enflame thyself with prayer."

HEALING THE HOME AND RELATIONS

Before we deal with the specifics of healing yourself or another person, it's a good idea to make sure the home is situated first. You can start by doing a banishing in each room and then using the cleansing and reversing floor washes and incenses that were covered in the chapter on home protection. After the house is clear you will want to work to provide a peaceful atmosphere using some of the following methods.

Scenting the Air

As you have probably been burning a great deal of incense during your defense, and then again to clear the house, I tend to stay away from peace incenses post-combat. If you do want to burn incense, I recommend very simple fragrances such as sandalwood, lavender, or a frankincense/myrrh combination. If you don't want to burn incense, a good way to establish a calm spiritual atmosphere is to place camphor blocks in the corners of the room, as camphor is known to calm down spirits while emitting only a minor scent. Placing potpourri herbs around the house is also a good method. I use a combination of cinnamon, pine, and sandalwood to help cultivate calm.

Peace Water

In New Orleans, a popular method for bringing peace to the home is said to have been invented by the famous "Voodoo Queen" Marie Laveau. It entails making a five-water wash that consists of rainwater, river water, spring water, ocean water, and holy water from a church. If you don't have access to one of these waters, it can be replaced by Florida water. This water can be used as a floor wash or simply sprinkled around the home. Another method of making peace water is simply layering oil and water in a bottle, the idea being that you are spreading anointing oil over troubled waters.

Sweetening Relations

One of the most common symptoms of magickal attack is relationship problems. If during the attack you experienced difficulties with your spouse, children, or others in your life, a good way to sweeten things up is to use a honey jar. All that is needed for this is a jar, lots of honey, a few sweets, such as molasses and sugar, and a personal item from each of the people who need relationship healing. It is best if everyone who is going to be linked to the bottle knows about the spell and gives their link over willingly, but it is not strictly necessary.

Place all the items in the jar and burn a white candle on top of the jar while saying:

By honey, sugar, and all things sweet,
Establish understanding and peace.

May good will reign between me and thee,
As I will, so shall it be.

Keep the jar in the bedroom if it is intended to heal relations between you and your spouse, and near the hearth if it is to work for your whole family. If sexual problems were caused by the attack, you can make one just for you and your partner and add sex fluids and pubic hairs to the jar as well as love items such as Adam and Eve root, pairs of bloodroot, Queen Elizabeth root, trillium, and the ever-popular raccoon penis bone.

HEALING THE INDIVIDUAL

After establishing an atmosphere of peace and good relations in which to convalesce, we must now set about tending to your own wounds. Just as we went back over the house with a floor wash and incense, you should also make sure every last remnant of your recent troubles is washed away in one of the spiritual cleansing and reversal baths that were given earlier in the book. You can also round out the elements by smoking yourself in one of the exorcism incenses given earlier or smudging yourself with sage. To do this, you can have someone else smoke you, or you can place the censer under a chair and let the smoke rise up around you as you meditate or just relax.

Relaxation

To combat feelings of anxiety and stress that often accompany magickal attack, I have found it beneficial to use the following relaxation methods. The first takes a bit of time and should be done once a day or so. Basically, all that needs to be done is each part of the body needs to be focused on piece by piece and willed to relax. Begin at the toes of the right foot. Focus on them and mentally tell them to relax. Feel them do so. Move to the toes of the left foot and do the same. Move to the left foot sole, do the same. The top of the left foot is next. Then the right sole. Then the top of the right foot. Then the left and right ankles.

Continue to move up the body, making sure that you get the front and back of each part. Go all the way up to the crown of the head. Take note of any resistance in your body to the command to relax. Spend some extra time on that area. If you like, you can visualize a golden healing light moving up the body wherever you are focusing, but this is not necessary. This entire process may take up to twenty or thirty minutes at first, but once you get the hang of it and become more relaxed in general, it will take only ten to fifteen minutes.

The second method I recommend for relaxation is very quick and can be used any time tension needs to be released. In this method, you tense up the entire body, starting from the toes up to the crown of the head. Allow this wave of willed tension to overtake you, and carry any tension you had prior to the exercise to join with it. Hold your entire body tense for a moment and then let it all go at once. Feel the tension leave your body and sink down into the Earth.

After you release the tension, inhale deeply, filling the lower chambers of the lungs first, then the upper chambers. Exhale, emptying the upper chambers, then the lower. This is called "vase breathing" because the lungs fill like vases filled with water. Take a few breaths like this and slowly take your mind off it, letting your breathing become more natural. This type of breathing is relaxing and brings many health benefits because it oxygenates the blood better than the short, shallow breaths we normally take.

Getting Right with Time

One of the more curious effects of some types of magickal attack is that it can put people out of step with time, which was mentioned in the first chapter. What I mean by this is that there is a natural rhythm to life and the healthy person is in harmony with this rhythm. A person out of harmony with this rhythm may find him- or herself constantly late for appointments, or too early for others. Missed opportunities abound, and you never seem to be in the right place at the right time. People will often say to you things such as, "If you had only arrived sooner," or "Too bad you left when you did."

There are various solutions to this problem, and in Tibet one of the reasons that so many laypeople take the Kalachakra[1] initiation, often thousands at a time, is that the empowerment is rumored to remedy this condition. A simpler method that I was taught is that at sunrise and sunset you should close your eyes and visualize a spinning swastika in your forehead surrounded by four other swastikas, which are also spinning. The swastika is a symbol of eternity that is used all over the planet, and its spinning is synched with the spinning of the entire universe. This simple and powerful meditation, if carried out as a daily practice for a period of a month or so, will put you right with time.

Healing Luck and Prosperity

There are some who believe that a person's luck and prosperity are parts of his or her psychic makeup and karma. As we discussed in the first chapter, one of the most prevalent complaints that cause people to think that they are under attack is a feeling of being jinxed. This jinxing of the luck can have a residual effect even after an attack, and, if after the attack is over you still feel that your luck and prosperity are suffering, you would be wise to employ methods specifically designed to increase them.

There is an enormous body of magickal spells and rituals that are designed to draw luck and money, and I encourage the reader to study the subject in depth. For now, I will include one three-ingredient bath and one three-ingredient conjure bag formula that will help fix your luck after an attack.

Luck/Prosperity Bath

Brew cinnamon, sassafras, and sugar into a tea and add it to your bathwater. Cinnamon draws money and luck, and drives away misfortune. Sassafras helps you hold onto what you come across, and sugar helps sweeten your condition in general.

Luck/Prosperity Conjure Hand

You will need one lucky hand root, one High John the Conqueror root, and cinnamon bark. The cinnamon is for drawing money. The lucky hand is for grabbing opportunity. High John is for cleverness and personal power. As per the instructions for mojo hands in the section on amulets, you should feed the hand with condition oil such as New Orleans Style Fast Luck Oil, which is made from oil of cinnamon, oil of vanilla, and wintergreen.[2]

Using Allies to Heal

If you have been making regular offerings to the gods, spirits, and world around you as instructed in the second chapter, then whether they have made themselves known to you or not, you have some powerful allies! I am not speaking here of specific spirits or familiars, but of the trees and rocks and rivers of the land where you live. Because of the bond that you have created through offering, they will be all too inclined to assist you in healing.

To do this type of healing you should go to a place in nature where you feel a particularly strong presence. An old tree, the ocean, or a large boulder are all good examples. Sit down and make yourself receptive to the energies of these places. Explain that you have been hurt and are in need of healing.

Through whatever means you have available, you should enter into trance. This can be done through intense drumming, breath control, self-hypnosis, meditation, and any combination of these and other methods. Once you have entered a trance, you should try to "enter" the spiritual dimension of the place where you are. The exact way to do this is impossible to explain as it is a function of the trance state, but you should try to find out for yourself. It is not as hard as it sounds. If you can't accomplish this in trance, you can try falling asleep in the place and entering its spiritual dimension through lucid dreaming.

Once you have entered the spiritual dimension, look for the genii of the local. The appearance of these spirits can differ greatly, but they are always at the center of things. Again, explain your situation and ask if the place can safely absorb your hurt. These places in nature can often take forces that trouble us and process them without harm to themselves as if they were food. What is poison to one being is not poison to all. If they agree, offer it up to the genii and thank them. Once you return to regular consciousness, you should make another offering, either in your own words or using the offering ceremony from the second chapter.

Healing Transference and Sacrifice

In many types of folk magick, serious cases of sickness can be transferred to animals, which are then sacrificed. In vodou this is most often done with a chicken, which is rubbed up and down the afflicted person's body while the sickness is lured out and into the chicken. Nepalese shamen called Jhankris do the same thing with an egg, placing it next to the afflicted part of a person's body and luring the damage out of the patient by drumming and chanting healing mantras.

You can use the egg method in self-healing. To do this you must pray fervently to the gods and call down the light of spirit into your body. You can use the conjuration of the column to do this, or simply imagine that a white purifying light descends from infinite space and enters through the crown of your head, filling your body with light, pushing physical and emotional disease out of your body as it does so. Take an egg and make a prayer to your deities. Rub the egg over yourself, starting from the head and moving down the body. This gives the sickness a place to go other than to resettle in the body.

When you are finished, you should take the egg someplace and bury it with respect. Just as if you had used a live chicken, what was once a potential life has done you a service by taking your disease into itself, sacrificing itself in the process. Even though it is just an egg, you should make an offering to the spirit of this potential life and commit it to the ground with respect and where the disease can be absorbed into Mother Earth.

Auric Healing

When the body, mind, and spirit are healthy, the aura of energy that surrounds a person is shaped like an egg that extends beyond the skin and several inches in all directions. Magickal and psychic attack can badly damage a person's aura and cause it to become misshapen. Even some healing techniques that remove an ill, such as the egg method, can leave a hole in the aura, just as a tumor removed from the skin leaves a scar that needs to fill and heal.

The best way to reshape the aura is to have a skilled healer or shaman do it for you. There are, however, methods that you can do yourself if you need to. To accomplish this, you need to set up a circle large enough for you to lie down in without touching the edges of the circle.

Begin in the northern quarter. Face outward and invoke powers of
the quarter:

I call upon the black bull of the North and the gods of night.
Rulers of the mountains and gnomish spirits,
Lords of Boreas, the northern wind,
And all ye princes of the powers of Earth,
I stir, summon, and call you.
I throw open the gate and call you to the circle
Grow forth and witness!

Move to the East and invoke:
I call upon the eagle of the East and the gods of the
        breaking day.

Rulers of wind and whirling sylphs,
Lords of Eurus, the eastern wind,
And all ye princes of the powers of air,
I stir, summon, and call you.
I throw open the gate and call you to the circle
Grow forth and witness!

Move to the South and invoke:
I call upon the lion of the Sun and the gods of noon.
Rulers of the desert and darting Djinn,
Powers of Notus, the southern wind,
I stir, summon, and call you.
I throw open the gate and call you to the circle
Grow forth and witness!

PROTECTION & REVERSAL MAGICK

Move to the West and invoke:
I call upon the water-bearers and gods of twilight.
Rulers of the deep and flowing undines,
Lords of Zephyrus the western wind,
And all ye princes of the powers of water,
I stir, summon, and call you.
I throw open the gate and call you to the circle
Grow forth and witness!

Having invoked the four quarters, you should now move to the center of the circle and face North. The reason that you are orienting the circle North instead of the usual East is that you are working with the magnetic fields rather than the movement of light and darkness. Invoke the powers of above and below:

I call upon the dove of the great heights and the serpent of
    the depths.
I throw open the powers of the sky!
I throw open the powers of the Earth!
I throw open the pylons of the heavens!
I throw open the pylons of the underworld!
I call the powers of the zenith and nadir to the circle
Grow forth and witness!
Lie down in the circle with your head in the North.
All ye powers of the heights
All ye powers of the depths
All ye powers of the horizon
I align myself with you.
May my own presence be in harmony with yours
As above so below
So mote it be.

Lie there for a while and allow the powers of the directions to magnetically adjust your energetic field. When you are finished, leave the circle in silence; there is no need to close.

The power of this rite rests in the age-old idea that man is, himself, a mirror image of the universe, and by invoking the macrocosm, your microcosm will be brought into line with it. Every time I perform this ritual, I find it amazingly powerful. It need not only be used after magickal attack but also can be employed any time you feel out of balance or sick.

Once, when I performed it after a particularly traumatic emotional blow, I was surprised to see actual beings moving in from the six directions and working on my aura to heal me. I am not promising these results for everyone, as it's not even the stated intent of the ritual, but I thought it worth mentioning.

SOUL RETRIEVAL

In the Judeo-Christian–influenced West, we tend to view the soul as a singular thing that you *are* at your core rather than as something that is itself made up of different parts. Not all cultures view it the same way, though, and instead see the soul as something that exists in several parts, some of which can be separated from the rest of the ego, causing great suffering and many emotional, psychic, and spiritual problems.

In ancient Egypt, for instance, a person was thought to be made up of a number of different parts. Apart from the Kha, or physical body, there is also the Ka, Ba, and Akh. The Ka is the psychological makeup of a person and is something of a double of the physical body after death and is generally bound to the lower planes. The Ba travels back and forth between the heavens and the Earth, and is what receives funerary offerings when they are made. The Akh, also called the Khu, is the complete opposite of the Kha in that it is the highest spiritual and eternal self.

In Tibet, they speak of the Namshe (rnam-shes) and the La (bla). The Namshe is the consciousness that reincarnates from life to life and carries the karma of an individual. The La is an emotional construct and is more connected to this particular incarnation and ego. It can leave the body under certain conditions and become fragmented, lost, or stolen. The Tibetans have many rituals for retrieving the La called La-gug.

In Haitian vodou the soul is also viewed as consisting of two parts: the Gros Bon Anj and Ti Bon Ang, which translate as "Big Good Angel" and "Little Good Angel," respectively.

The Gros Bon Anj is what travels to heaven when you die and is connected ultimately to God. The Ti Bon Ang is somewhat like the Tibetan La and is connected to you as an individual. Like the La, the Ti Bon Ang can be lost, fragmented, or stolen. It is the Ti Bon Ang that is captured and controlled in the famous rites of zombification.

Victor and Cora Anderson's Feri tradition of witchcraft divides up the soul into three parts called Sticky One, Shining Body, and Paraclete. Sticky One is the animal and child nature that somewhat corresponds to the Freudian id. Shining Body is the intellect and mental capacity, extending from the rational and logical to the psychic and energetic levels. The Paraclete is pure spirit and represents your own divinity, connecting you to ancestors and gods and universe as a whole.

The 7th-century "Cauldron of Poesy," a Bardic poem from Ireland, tells of three cauldrons that make up the soul in the Celtic traditions. Multiple souls are also encountered in Hermetics, Kabbalah, and Sufism. Whatever system of soul anthropology (literally the study of what makes a human) to which you ascribe, most agree that there is some aspect of the self that can be separated from the rest and must therefore be retrieved if the persona is to be made whole again.

In general, a soul becomes separated through one of three ways. It can be shaken loose through some trauma or shock, it can be driven away by overwhelming shame and guilt, or it can be stolen through occult means. Each of these three situations requires a different method of remedy to bring the soul back in line with the rest of the self. Soul retrieval is complex work and, like exorcism, is best left to specialists in that field. Unfortunately, experts in the field are few and far between and you should at least know a little bit about what is necessary in each of these three cases. In each of these, I will be talking in terms of recovering the soul for someone else. If you feel that you need soul retrieval done, then you must get another person to do it for you, as you will be in no condition to do the work. Such is the nature of the job.

When the soul is shaken loose by trauma or shock, the severity of the situation can vary in degrees that are directly related to how severe and prolonged the trauma was. For instance, a soul can be shaken loose by a short and sharp physical pain, such as you might experience in a car accident. It can also be caused by emotional shock, as when you find out that a lover leaves you or a family member has unexpectedly died. If you have ever experienced the disorientation and numbness that can accompany these experiences, then you know what it is like to lose part of your soul temporarily. Thankfully, the effect is usually temporary, and the soul lingers nearby until it is drawn back into the body by nature.

If the soul does not return automatically, the best method for retrieval is simply to make the host body as relaxed and carefree as possible so the soul finds it to be the most desirable place to be.

Ceremonies involving pleasurable sensations such as massage and feasting can be constructed to attempt to lure the soul back.

Cases of prolonged trauma result in more dire situations. Prisoners of war or children who have suffered abuse over a long period are not likely to have their souls lingering nearby, waiting to come back in. In these cases, the soul is usually hiding somewhere near where it was lost. Often it is near water or a tall tree, as these are primal scenes that are comforting to our spirits. In these cases the witch must first repair any psychic and energetic damage to the body as well as possible, such as with the aura repairing ceremony on pages 171–174. In cases such as this, the patient should also be under the care of a mental-healthcare professional who can deal with the psychological problems that arose from the trauma. This will also prepare the body to receive the returning soul.

The actual retrieval of the soul in this case is more difficult than just making the victim relaxed. In these cases, the witch must rely on the gods and her spiritual allies to seek the soul and lead it back. Alternatively, the witch must travel in the spirit him- or herself and look for the soul, and ask it to come back. If you have the capacity to do this, and you find the soul, you simply gather it up into your arms and return to your own body. The soul can be returned to its owner by holding out your hands and blowing the soul gently back into the person's heart.

In cases where the soul has been driven away because of some great shame or guilt, the toughest part of the problem is getting the person to deal with the cause. Often it is some immoral action that he has justified in his rational mind, but which he secretly finds abhorrent deep down. The conflict has literally driven the soul from the body and, before it is retrieved, the conflict must be resolved. Generally, this is done through one of two methods: either the person makes a confession and comes to terms with her actions, thus realizing that her deep feeling was correct and that she was wrong; or the person realizes that the act wasn't really immoral at all and that her deep mind was reacting out of social training rather than a real sense of right and wrong. For instance, in the first case, someone who beat or killed someone without provocation may be able to rationalize it to himself by any number of means, but deep down he knows that it was an immoral action. This person will need to confess and come to terms with this in order to retrieve his soul. In the second case, someone who engages in homosexual sex may know rationally that there is nothing wrong with it morally, and that he is just following his natural inclination, yet still suffer from deep religious and social programming that tells him he is committing a heinous act. In this case, the deep mind must be brought into line with rational thinking in order for the self to be made healthy and able to accept the soul. After the guilt or shame is resolved, the soul can be retrieved in exactly the same fashion as stated previously.

I again want to point out that I am not a psychiatric professional, and unless you are, someone suffering soul loss due to intense guilt and shame should be under the care of a professional. Do not pretend to be something that you are not, or you will cause more problems than you solve.

In the last case, where the soul is stolen by another witch or magician, we have a very serious problem indeed. The soul must be found and taken back by force. Because a magician that engages in this type of magick will usually have to bind the soul to a physical object, you can go and find and retrieve the object if you know who has stolen it. The methods that you use to do this are up to you and can involve the various methods of counter-magick that were provided in the last chapter, or by more serious means. All I want to say is that nothing I write in this book is intended to encourage illegal activities, so if you feel compelled to enter another person's temple, looking for a soul trap, that's on you.

If you can't get at the place where the soul is kept or don't know who has it, it can still be retrieved by divine intercession. You must make a petition to your deity on behalf of the afflicted person and humbly yet frankly demand that they retrieve and restore the soul even if it brings harm or death to the person who stole it.

If working with Hekate, for instance, you could use the following charge.

> Hail, many-named mother of the gods, whose children
>   are fair.
> Hail, mighty Hekate of the threshold, keyholder of
>   the world.
> Hail, Enodia, keeper of the crossroads and three ways.
> Nether, Nocturnal, and Infernal one,
> You who walk disheveled and wild through tombs and
>   cremation grounds
> Cloaked in saffron, crowned with oak leaves and coils
>   of serpents
> You who are followed by hordes of ghosts, dogs, and
>   restless spirits
> Yet are at once the luminous Empress of Empyrian realms.
> I come to you for aid.
> Hekate Chthonia, Queen of Witches
> A soul has been wrongfully stolen.
> You who are the supreme mistress of bindings and sorceries
> Who are serpent-haired and serpent-girdled
> And whose womb is covered in serpent scales
> I come to you for justice.
> You are greater than any worldly sorcerer

As you lead Demeter through Hades with the light of your
 twin torches
Lead the soul back to (name of victim)
Propolos, steer the soul back to its home.
Propylaia, guard it from further dangers and damage.
Phosphoros, light the path with your twin torches.
Kourotropos, deliver the soul to (name of victim)
 as you would deliver a child to its mother.
When you return we will rejoice and sing your praise.
Hail, many-named mother of the gods, whose children
 are fair.
Hail, mighty Hekate of the threshold, keyholder of
 the world.

If Hekate is successful, both you and the patient should make an offering to her as described elsewhere in this book.

Whatever the causes and conditions of the soul loss, I want to again urge you to attempt it yourself only after you have exhausted all other options. It is best if you can work within the worldview of the client as well. A person who practices vodou and believes a bokor has stolen her soul will respond best to methods used by a houngan or mambo. A Buddhist will respond best to methods used by a lama. A Christian will respond best to methods used by a priest or minister. All of these professionals receive training that is well beyond what can be presented in a short book such as this.

A wise witch knows his limits and works within them.

NEW EDITION COMMENTARY

This is probably the most neglected chapter in the book. I never get asked about it. The problem is that it is one of the most important chapters. If you have been through a genuine magickal or psychic attack, you need time to heal and regather your energies. Even if you have successfully defended yourself, you still may have a gaping wound that needs to heal.

My strong advice is that after a serious magickal attack you do nothing for a month. No magick, no meditation, no psychic work. Nothing. Just rest. Netflix and chill.

If you need healing, try the methods in this book, and if you need more serious healing than this, see a specialist. Whether it's standard medical/psychological medicine or alternative therapies, healing is an area of specialization that should be respected.

Chapter 9

FINAL WORDS

I have already said that magickal, psychic, and spiritual attacks happen more frequently than even most occultists like to admit. I will go one step further: they happen every day and to everyone. They are launched not only by offended spirits and malicious magicians, but by major corporations and political parties. Where does a magickal seal of binding end and a corporate logo start? Where does the use of neurolinguistic programming in sales end and the use of sorcerous bindings begin? At this point in history, the most advanced techniques of psychic manipulation and hypnosis are being employed against you in an effort to control how you behave, what you buy, and what you think. If you haven't thought of this as magick, then think again.

The methods I included in this book hopefully will serve as armor not only against ancient spells and curses, but also against these more accepted, yet in many ways more insidious, modes of binding and control. In particular, I hope that the three daily practices of banishing, meditation, and offering will change you enough that these powers begin to lose their hold. Taking back your attention is perhaps the most revolutionary act one can perform in today's world, and all the techniques in this book can be used as tools toward accomplishing this goal.

As to the more traditionally occult attacks that are the main focus of this book, I have attempted to provide a useful survey that covers many different modes of practice. Some traditionalists will accuse me of being too eclectic in my methods. Those used to ceremonial magick may be put off by the folk magick. Those comfortable with hoodoo may not find resonance with the visualization techniques. Those expecting a book on standard modern Wicca may be turned off by just about everything I wrote!

I was eclectic in my choices for a reason. We no longer live in a purely traditional culture. Modern modes of communication and travel have made the world much smaller than it was. The chance that a Santero or Peruvian shaman will cross paths with a Jewish Kabbalist or British witch is now a very real possibility. In fact, it happens all the time. Without going out of my way to seek anyone out specifically, I was exposed to a Rosicrucian teacher, a rootworker, a Santera, a Buddhist ngakpa, and several different Wiccans all within central New Jersey, and all before I was twenty years old!

These different traditions of magick each emphasize different points, and what works as a defense against one may not work as a defense against another. Someone who relied solely on the Golden Dawn's Lesser Banishing Ritual of the Pentagram or the OTO's Star Ruby may find his defenses breached easily by someone laying Goofer Dust in his shoes. Similarly, someone who relies too heavily on red brick dust and amulets may find himself vulnerable to the attacks of Goetic demons summoned by the ceremonialist.

Magick works on a number of different levels: the physical and near-physical etheric levels; the astral and energetic levels; and the mental and purely divine levels. Different world traditions of magick emphasize different levels. For example, hoodoo and other types of folk magick place great emphasis on the physical level through the use of material objects, such as powders and charms, and also on the divine level through the use of prayer to consecrate these items. Hoodoo doesn't focus as much on the energetic and astral levels, though that is not to say that it doesn't use them at all. Ceremonial magick, meanwhile, places great emphasis on energetic levels that can be seen in rituals where pentagrams or hexagrams are traced in the air; other than the tools of ceremony, it is not as concerned with physical magick as folk magick is. In a world where you can encounter any type of magickal practitioner without traveling very far at all, it is necessary to be able to defend yourself on all these levels.

Still, I do not want my eclecticism to come off as dilettantism, as so much of the modern eclectic works tend to do. To this end, I have included an appendix with sources for delving further into different traditions within their own framework and cultural milieu. I have received fairly orthodox training in each of the traditions that I have drawn from and been inspired by, and I want to pay homage and respect to each of these in their own context.

The methods presented should be enough for you to identify and mount a defense against any type of occult attack that you may encounter. There remains the possibility, however, that no matter what you do, you may be outgunned, overwhelmed, or just up against something or someone with much more power and experience than you have. If you find your defenses crumbling, there is no shame in seeking help from either a group or a professional worker of some kind.

If you do seek outside help, make sure that the people you turn to have a good reputation in the community and are good at what they do. If it's a professional that you need, then make sure that he or she doesn't try to charge you an arm and a leg for his or her services. Reasonable fees differ, depending on the situation, and you should be prepared to pay something similar to what you would pay any other professional such as a doctor. If the worker is charging hundreds and hundreds of dollars, while not showing any sign that they are actually doing work, then you should cut ties immediately and look elsewhere. Some psychic readers make a living on convincing people that they have been cursed and charging exorbitant rates to have the curse removed.

The reader will note that the book provides specific spells for some things, and only general guidance on others. This is because more than just a grammar of defensive spells, I am hoping to provide an overall strategy and framework for dealing with attacks that can be used by anyone in any situation. In working for myself, my friends, and my clients, I have never run across the exact same situation twice, and so I want my readers to be able to use this guide to design a custom-made defense to any attack that they may come across.

Magickal attack can be a horrible thing to suffer. When witches and magicians are increasingly denying that it happens, where does one turn? When books that purport to train people in witchcraft will not even mention anything specific about curses and attack, how are readers to know what to do in defense?

In a world where an unprecedented amount of people are being guided through the maze of witchcraft and magick primarily through books, it is my hope that this book can fill in some of these holes in training and provide a resource for people to rely on should trouble rear its head.

It is significant that I am finishing this book on Candlemas, the time when people traditionally light candles against the darkness.

If this book can serve as a candle that dispels doubt, difficulty, and danger for even a few people, then its purpose will have been fulfilled.

May all beings have happiness
and the causes of happiness.
May all beings be free from suffering
and the causes of suffering.
May all beings never be separated from the
happiness that knows no suffering.
May all beings live in equanimity,
free from attachment and aversion.

Inominandum, Candlemas 2006

Appendix A

HEKATE

Hekate is a deeply mysterious and misunderstood goddess. Most people tend to have a single-minded view of her, best exemplified by her appearance in Shakespeare's *Macbeth*: as a goddess of darkness and black magick. Recently, Neo-Pagans have attempted to clear away this nefarious reputation but unfortunately went even further from the truth, painting her as a crone goddess of the moon. Although Hekate was propitiated as a goddess of black magick during some stages, and was connected with the moon in later Roman representations, she was *never* portrayed as a crone. Indeed, Hekate is always portrayed as a young goddess.

The name Hekate has many meanings, the most accepted being "Far Darting" or "Far Removed." Hekate is believed to have her origins as an eastern great-goddess from Anatolia or Karia. Her first appearance in Greek literature is in the *Theogony of Hesiod* and the *Hymn to Demeter* where she is not a lunar or dark goddess at all, but rather an illuminator and guardian. The *Theogony* describes her as a titan that sided with the gods and is thus afforded numerous powers and domains, such as goddess of games and a nursemaid, amongst other things. In the *Hymn to Demeter* she seems almost Solar in nature. Indeed when she witnesses Persephone being taken into Hades, she is with Helios, the god of the Sun. She then illuminates the path of Demeter into Hades with her twin torches.

Far from a crone, it is because of her youthful form she was believed to take the place of the young women that would be sacrificed to protect a city from harm. Such was the case with Agamemnon's daughter Iphigenia, who was sacrificed to protect the Greek fleet on its way to Troy. By possessing them at the last moment, she saved the young women the agony of death.

Beginning around the 5th century BC, she begins to develop her chthonic underworld element as well as her connection to witchcraft. It is believed by some that she became identified with the goddess of Pherai in Thessaly, who was also called Enodia, indicating that she is a goddess of the crossroads. Apart from her youthful human form, she appears in some literature as being worshiped in forms that incorporate animal heads, such as lions, serpents, and dogs. Because of her connection to crossroads as well as her interest in women that die before their time, she got a reputation for being a goddess of witchcraft and the dead around this time. She is invoked in this chthonic aspect often in the Greek Magical Papyri and in the famous lead defixiones curse tablets.

In the 2nd century AD she appears in the Chaldean Oracles as a transcendent and mystical goddess, with hardly any of her chthonic associations still attached. She is the wife of Had, the first father, and also Hadit, the second father, and thus is both manifest and unmanifest at the same time.

She is invoked as the patron of this book because she has been identified as a goddess used in both defensive and offensive magick—a goddess both of darkness and of light. Her image, called a Hekataion, was once so prevalent as a defensive amulet that it was mentioned by Aristophanes in the *Wasps* as being on every door in Athens, thus making her an excellent choice as a protector. Her darker and more sinister aspects were often invoked by those seeking justice, and thus she makes an ideal goddess for reversing and counter-magick work.

Since this book was written, interest in Hekate has grown immensely, and there are now countless books, groups, and web pages available. My favorite three books for beginners are:

- *Hekate Liminal Rites: A Study of the Rituals, Magic and Symbols of the Torch-Bearing Triple Goddess of the Crossroads* by David Rankine and Sorita d'Este

- *Hekate in Ancient Greek Religion* by Rob Von Rudloff

- *The Goddess Hekate* by Stephen Ronan

All three books focus on Hekate's origins and history. From there you can move outward into more historical sources, or forward into modern sources, with a firm foundation in her history.

The rituals in this book are related to a larger arcana of magick centered on Hekate known as the Sorcery of Hekate Training. You can find out more about this specific way of working with Hekate on my website.

Appendix B

HEKATE DAILY DEVOTIONAL

In the chapter on regular practice, I noted that daily banishing rituals are not necessarily desirable, especially if you want to communicate more readily with spirits as part of your overall practice. Banishings are still recommended for times when you feel you are under attack or potentially faced with more dangerous forces than usual, but not as an everyday thing. I recommend a regular devotional practice instead. The following short rite and chant will serve you very well in this regard.

HAIL, MANY-NAMED MOTHER OF THE GODS,
    WHOSE CHILDREN ARE FAIR
HAIL, MIGHTY HEKATE OF THE THRESHOLD,
    KEYHOLDER OF THE WORLD
HAIL TO THEE, ENODIA, KEEPER OF THE FOUR-
    AND THREE-WAY CROSSROADS
NETHER, NOCTURNAL, AND INFERNAL ONE

I BECKON TO YOU
  GRANT ME THE PLEASURE OF YOUR PRESENCE
NIGHT MOTHER! SAVIOR! MISTRESS OF
  SOLITUDE!
LADY OF LIGHT, AND THE DARKNESS THAT
  CONTAINS IT
YOU WHO WALK DISHEVELED AND WILD
  THROUGH TOMBS AND CREMATION
  GROUNDS
CLOAKED IN SAFFRON, CROWNED WITH OAK
  LEAVES AND COILS OF SERPENTS
YOU WHO ARE FOLLOWED BY HORDES OF
  GHOSTS, DOGS, AND RESTLESS SPIRITS
YET ARE ALSO THE LUMINOUS EMPRESS OF THE
  EMPYRIAN REALMS.
I BECKON TO YOU
  GRANT ME THE PLEASURE OF YOUR PRESENCE
KLEIDOKHOUS, GRANT ME THE KEY TO THE
  MYSTERIES
PROPYLAIA, THROW OPEN THE GATE
PHOSPHOROS, LIGHT MY WAY WITH YOUR
  TWIN TORCHES OF MERCY AND SEVERITY
PROPOLOS, STEER ME SAFELY THROUGH THE
  FOUR RIVERS
BRIMO, SHAKE THE PILLARS OF PERCEPTION
  WITH YOUR WRATH
PHYSIS, BIND ALL DEMONS AND SET THEM
  INTO MY SERVICE
KLEIDOKHOUS, GRANT ME THE KEY TO THE
  MYSTERIES

ANASSA ENEROI, QUEEN OF THE DEAD,
    ALLOW ME CONTACT WITH MY ANCESTORS.
HEKATE CHTHONIA, QUEEN OF SORCERY
TEACHER OF HOWLINGS AND BINDINGS
INSTRUCT ME IN THE MYSTERIES
MAY THE THREE FATES FAVOR ME
MAY THE THREE GRACES BLESS ME
MAY THE THREE GORGONS PROTECT ME
MAY THE THREE FURIES AVENGE ME
MAY THE THREE-FACED GODDESS,
SERPENT-HAIRED, SERPENT-GIRDLED,
    WITH WOMB OF SERPENT SCALES
    BE HERE NOW WITH MY SPIRIT!

Repeat the following mantra as many times as possible. One hundred times minimum; one thousand times is preferable.

IO HEKA IO HO

When you feel that the presence of Hekate has been evoked and stabilized into your sphere through the call and the mantra, you can move on to the offerings. This can be as simple as rubbing your hands together and offering the heat from your hands, or can involve a simple offering of incense and libation poured into the ground. This is a daily practice, so keep it simple.

I THANK YOU, HEKATE, FOR YOUR PRESENCE
    AND BLESSING.
    AND FOR THE BLESSINGS YOU HAVE GIVEN
I GIVE OFFERING AND PRAISE TO YOU IN ALL
    YOUR FORMS

I GIVE OFFERING AND THANKS TO THE
UNTIMELY DEAD WHO FOLLOW YOU
I GIVE OFFERING AND THANKS TO THE
SPIRITS UNDER YOUR COMMAND
MAY ALL BE PLEASED. MAY ALL BE AT PEACE.
EGO SE ETELESA
CHAIRO !

Appendix C

EXORCISM OF TWIN TORCHES

As noted in Chapter 5 on exorcism, I decided to deliver a short example of an exorcism script dedicated to Hekate. This is just an example and will need to be repeated multiple times or expanded upon by the exorcist.

There are several key features common to exorcism scripts that I wish to bring to your attention:

1. Links to historical or mythological events. Catholic exorcisms recall acts of saints, or events from the Gospels, then relate them to the problem at hand—exorcising a spirit. In this text I draw upon Hekate's role in overthrowing the titans, her leading Demeter through the underworld, her slaying of the gigantes, and her role in the Chaldean Oracles, and tell the spirit why these are reasons to obey.

2. Invocation of powerful associated spirits. In this case the guardians from the Sphere of Hekas and sets of female

triads from Greek mythology. These have an almost "surrounding" effect on a troublesome spirit.

3. Invocation of different epitaphs or names of the central deity. There is a time-honored idea that certain names or powers are more effective at thwarting certain spirits. Knowing which name is most effective at thwarting which spirit is not easy to know ahead of time, which is why before the Catholic Church standardized the *Rituale Romanum,* priests would have volumes of different exorcisms at their disposal. This exorcism calls upon epitaphs of Hekate in alliterative groups of three. There are other longer exorcisms dedicated to her that contain one hundred names.

Please use this with great care and respect. If you are using it to free a patient of obsession or possession, a few other people should be in the room to bear witness. Possessed or obsessed patients sometimes become physically violent during exorcisms, and would-be exorcists have sometimes committed abuse under the umbrella of exorcism. People trained in treating mental health issues and upholding legal standards of care should absolutely be present for your protection and the protection of the afflicted.

> OH, SPIRIT WHO IS OPPRESSING X (name of
>   afflicted person or place)
> I EXORCISE AND BIND YOU IN THE NAME OF
>   HEKATE,
> WHO HOLDS SWAY OVER THE OLD GODS AND
>   THE NEW
> AS ZEUS CALLED ON HEKATE
> TO GAIN DOMINION OVER THE TITANS,

I CLAIM DOMINION OVER YOU, (insert name of
spirit if you know it)
THROUGH HER POWER.

AS DEMETER CALLED ON HEKATE TO REVEAL
PERSEPHONE'S FATE,
AND OVERCOME THE TRIALS OF THE
UNDERWORLD,
I CALL ON HER TO NAME YOU, (spirit X),
AND OVERCOME ALL YOUR POWER.

AS HEKATE SLEW THE GIGANTES CLYTIUS WITH
HER TWIN FIRE BRANDS,

SHE CASTS YOU OUT, (spirit X),
AS SHE MOVES EFFORTLESSLY BETWEEN THE
FORMLESS, AND THE FORMED WORLDS OF
HAD AND HADAD,
THERE IS NO REFUGE FROM HER LIGHT

BY THE SECRET NAMES AKTIPHIS, ERESHKIGAL,
NEBOTOSOALETH
YOU ARE CHASED FROM THE REALMS OF THE
LIVING, THE DEAD,
AND THE DREAMING AND YOU ARE BOUND
HERE BEFORE ME.

BY HEKATE'S DIVINE BREATH AND BY ABAEK'S
FLASHING SWORDS
YOU ARE CHASED FROM THE AIR

BY HEKATE'S FIERY SPIRIT AND BY PYRHUM'S
   FLAMING BREATH YOU
ARE CHASED FROM THE FIRE

BY HEKATE'S BOILING BLOOD AND BY ERMITI'S
   POISON CHALICE YOU
ARE DRIVEN FROM THE WATER

BY HEKATE'S INCORRUPTABLE FLESH AND BY
   DIMGALI'S SHACKLES
YOU ARE DRIVEN FROM THE EARTH

THERE IS NO SPHERE THAT IS BEYOND HER
   REACH
THERE IS NO PLACE THAT CAN GRANT YOU
   REFUGE FROM HER COMMAND

I EXORCISE YOU, (spirit X), THAT YOU WITH-
   DRAW FROM (x) NEVER TO RETURN.

IF YOU DO NOT LISTEN AND OBEY THIS
   INSTANCE
YOU WILL BE CHASED CEASELESSLY BY
   HEKATE'S HOARD

AS ALL TRIADS BELONG TO HER YOU ARE
   THRICE EXORCISED
AND BOUND
BY A PENTAGRAM OF TRIADS YOU ARE
   EXORCISED AND BOUND!
THE SIRENS BEWITCH YOU WITH THEIR SONG

THE FATES BIND YOU WITH THEIR THREAD
THE GORGONS PETRIFY YOU WITH THEIR GAZE
THE HARPIES STEAL SUSTENANCE WITH THEIR
  CLAWS
THE FURIES RIP YOU FROM (x) AND CARRY YOU
  OFF TO TARTARUS IN CHAINS
IN THE NAME OF HEKATE TRIMORPHOS
I CAST YOU OUT!
IN THE NAME OF HEKATE HEXACHEIRA I CAST
  YOU OUT!
IN THE NAME OF HEKATE SOTERIA I CAST
  YOU OUT!
BY TRIMORPHOS! TRIONYMOS!
  TRIPHTHOGGOS!
YOU ARE BOUND!
BY PROPOLOS! PROPYLIA! PROTHYRAEA!
YOU ARE CONSTRAINED!
BY AOROIBOROS! AOROIDAMNIA!
  AOROIANAXSIA!
YOU ARE SUBDUED!
BY DAMNAMENE! DAMNASENEIA!
  DAMNODANIA!
YOU WILL OBEY!
BY NYKTERIA! NYKTIPHANIA! NYKTIBOOS!
YOU ARE EXORCISED!
BY PASIPHAESSA! PASIMEDOUSA!
  PASIMEDEONSA!
YOU ARE CAST FROM (x) AND SHALL GO TO (y)
  (wherever you expect the spirit to run to)
IT IS DONE!

Notes

PREFACE

1. Letter #8 from Robert Cochrane to the ceremonial magician William Gray.

CHAPTER 1

1. *WorldNetDaily.com* (July 26, 2005).
2. Dion Fortune, *Psychic Self-Defense* (Samuel Weiser, 2001).
3. David J. Hufford, *The Terror That Comes in the Night: An Experience-Centered Study of Supernatural Assault Traditions* (University of Pennsylvania Press, 1982).
4. Which is neither by Albertus Magnus, nor has any Egyptian magick in it, but is nonetheless an interesting collection of folk magick that is still in use.

CHAPTER 2

1. The central channel, also called the Shushumna or Avadhuti, runs from the crown of the head down through the body and is the center post of the subtle body, just as the spine is for the physical body. It is only one of many thousands of nadis. Two other important nadis that run alongside the center channel are Ida and Pingala, the masculine and feminine channels.
2. They are in fact part of a larger collection of material on Hekate that I have been working with for several years now.
3. Aleister Crowley, *Liber Tzaddi.*
4. My thanks to Tau Nemesius for teaching me these mudras associated with IAO from the Russian traditions of gnostic magick.
5. There are other interpretations of this formula worth noting. The Golden Dawn viewed IAO as an acronym for Isis, Apophis, Osiris, and thus a formula for creation, destruction, and rebirth.

CHAPTER 3

1. See Chapter 7 on reversals and counter-magick.
2. For a fuller treatment of iron's protective properties, see the excellent essay "The apotropaic use of iron" by B. Gendler (*www.panikon.com/phurba/articles/iron/html*).
3. The three metals are Nam Chak, Sa Chak, and Dri Chak. Nam Chak is sky metal from meteorites, Sa Chak is metal from the Earth, and Dri Chak is metal that has been taken from a sword or knife that has killed someone.
4. Under no circumstances am I recommending that you dig up a grave for human bones or coffin nails. They can be purchased

legally if you look hard enough and there can be serious spiritual, not to mention legal, ramifications of disturbing graves.

5. A full treatment of mojo bags is beyond the scope of this work. Interested parties should check out the work of catherine yronwode, the proprietor of the Lucky Mojo Curio Company.

6. Note that the word devil in folk magick isn't always referring to an evil presence, but can be making reference to the crossroads gods of Africa or the many-horned gods of Europe and the varying degrees to which these figures have been identified with the Devil. In fact, there are many witch traditions in Europe that embrace the label of the Devil onto the Horned God and have no problem with Robin being called such.

7. Mary Alicia Owen, "Voodoo Tales as Told among the Negroes of the Southwest: Collected from Original Sources," *Missouri Folklore Society Journal* (v. 8–9, 1986–87).

CHAPTER 4

1. Witch's salt, or black salt, is salt with soot or some other agent added to it to turn it black.

2. The Golden Dawn made extensive use of these quotes in their Watchtower Ceremony. As an example, when circulating the element Earth through the temple you would invoke: "Stoop not down into the darkly splendid world wherein continually lieth a faithless depth and Hades wrapped in gloom, delighting in unintelligible images, precipitous, winding; a black ever-rolling abyss ever espousing a body unluminous, formless and void."

3. I would like to suggest that if you collect graveyard dirt, that you do it during the day or, at the very least, do it at

a graveyard that is open all day and night. There is no law against leaving a dime and collecting some dirt from a grave, and people generally don't get very nosy about what others are doing at a graveyard. There are, however, laws against trespassing, and there is no compelling reason to collect graveyard dirt at night, especially for protective reasons.

4. This combination is from a famous couplet "Trefoil, Vervail, Saint John's Wort Dill/Hinder Witches of their Will." Trefoil is any three-sided leaf, such as clover.

5. This is not to say that Nagas are evil by nature. They are not; in fact, they are often propitiated and used in Himalayan sorcery and shamanism. Certain Nagas, however, can cause problems if angered, thus the function of the Garuda.

6. Not to be confused with the Eleocharis dulcis, which is what is commonly served in Chinese restaurants as a water chestnut.

7. Hand gestures.

8. Contrary to popular belief, the Goetia does not call for the triangle to be used for all the spirits it lists, only the most rebellious amongst them. There are three that are listed as specifically needing the triangle.

9. The various names here are names of specific harmful spirits from Greek mythology. The Empusae, Lamia, and Mormo, for instance, are spirits who feed on children. The Vrykolakas is a vampire. The Apotropaioi are ghosts and all kinds of restless dead. *Kakodaemon* literally means "evil spirit" and is a catchall.

CHAPTER 6

1. Carl McColman, "Is Wicca Under a Spell?" *www.beliefnet.com* (2005).

2. Those interested in a full response to this attitude should see my article "Spell Casting: The Witches' Craft," which can be read on *witchesofthecraft.com*.
3. Also known as the Lesser Key of Solomon.
4. Philadelphia's OTO Body.
5. Of course, not all the dharmapalas had to be pressed into service. Some offered their services to the Dharma and were thus thought of as being especially benevolent. One such spirit is Dorje Lekpa, whose name literally means "Thunderbolt Good Guy."
6. The four schools of Tibetan Buddhism—the Nyingma, Kagyu, Sakya, and Gelugpa—did not always get along.
7. I personally find Carapelli Olive Oil bottles ideal for this spell, but any bottle will do.
8. Gematria is the Kabbalistic art whereby words are reduced to their numerical values and associated with other words.
9. Alexandra David-Néel, *Magic and Mystery in Tibet* (University Books, 1965).
10. I have been studying Tibetan Tantra and magick for many years now both in America and in Nepal, and have never heard the term *culpa* referred to in this manner. Instead, it refers to beings in the retinue of Tantric deities that are visualized/invoked in generation stage Tantra. Whether she understood the term correctly or not, we can learn a valuable lesson from her experience.
11. See Agrippa's Three Books of Occult Philosophy for these planetary symbols and times.
12. *www.WorldNetDaily.com* (July 26, 2005).

CHAPTER 7

1. This phrase is Sumerian and means "Begone, go to the Desert!"
2. These are all names of rivers in Hades. The last, the Lethe, is the river of forgetfulness and indicates not only that the target has been swept away, but that you can forget him completely.

CHAPTER 8

1. *Kalachakra* literally means "Wheel of Time" and refers to a whole set of rituals, Tantric yogas, medical texts, and prophecies. The legend of Shangrila is derived from the Kalachakra prophecies that foretell the sacred spiritual kingdom manifesting physically in the future in order to defeat Muslims in a world war.
2. This oil formula is taken from the anthropologist and rootworker Zora Neale Hurston in her excellent book *Mules and Men* (Harper & Row, 1990).

　　　　PROTECTION & REVERSAL MAGICK

About the Author

 Jason Miller (Inominandum) has devoted thirty-five years to studying practical magick in its many forms. He is the author of six books, including the now classic *Protection & Reversal Magick*. He teaches several courses online including the Strategic Sorcery One Year Course, the Sorcery of Hekate Training, and the Black School of Saint Cyprian. He lives with his wife and children in the mountains of Vermont. Find out more at *StrategicSorcery.net*.

To Our Readers

Weiser Books, an imprint of Red Wheel/Weiser, publishes books across the entire spectrum of occult, esoteric, speculative, and New Age subjects. Our mission is to publish quality books that will make a difference in people's lives without advocating any one particular path or field of study. We value the integrity, originality, and depth of knowledge of our authors.

Our readers are our most important resource, and we appreciate your input, suggestions, and ideas about what you would like to see published.

Visit our website at *www.redwheelweiser.com,* where you can learn about our upcoming books and free downloads, and also find links to sign up for our newsletter and exclusive offers.

You can also contact us at *info@rwwbooks.com* or at

Red Wheel/Weiser, LLC
65 Parker Street, Suite 7
Newburyport, MA 01950